A Question of Values

Morris Berman

ISBN: 1-4537-2288-2
ISBN-13: 9781453722886

For Peter Boltz

Contents

Books by Morris Berman

Social Change and Scientific Organization

Trilogy on human consciousness:

The Reenchantment of the World
Coming to Our Senses
Wandering God: A Study in Nomadic Sprituality

Trilogy on the American empire:

The Twilight of American Culture
Dark Ages America: The Final Phase of Empire
Why America Failed: The Roots of Imperial Decline

A Question of Values (essays)

Counting Blessings (poetry)

Destiny (fiction)

We would rather be ruined than changed

—W.H. Auden, *The Age of Anxiety*

Preface

In 2006, after considerable thought on my part, I left the United States and moved to Mexico. This was not just a reaction to the government of Dick Cheney and George Bush. Indeed, I saw them as symptomatic of a whole way of life, a whole system of values, and it was that that I wished to leave behind. Nor, in my opinion, is the government of Barack Obama very different, except in matters of style. In substance, America is still dominated by corporate and military values; by a pathetic philosophy of "We're No. 1!"; and by a way of life that is aggressive and competitive down to its very roots. This is not to say that Mexico is not without serious social and political problems; I am no starry-eyed romantic on that score. But Mexico has a very large, beating heart, and a graciousness that is part of the air that Mexicans breathe. America, I felt, had no heart; it was a callous place, with a death instinct hanging over it like a huge dark cloud. Nor are Americans very gracious to one another, by and large. Indeed, they seem to me to be anxious, angry, and depressed, and have no time for the common courtesies that make a society work. The place, in a word, was and is toxic; it is making its citizens ill, both physically and spiritually; it is a nation from which the human dimension of life has largely been purged. Several decades ago, Adlai Stevenson described it as a "chaotic, selfish, indifferent commercial society" dominated by an "inner, purposeless tyranny of a confused and aimless way of life." Twenty-odd years later, Jimmy Carter said much the same thing, in an attempt to get Americans to come to terms with the emptiness of their lives. It was a futile effort, and it seems clear enough that this description of America in the fifties, and in 1979, applies even more to the country now than it did thirty or fifty years ago. On a human level, we seem to be a lot worse off. I asked myself if I wanted to grow old in such an environment, bereft of friendship and community, and the answer was a loud and resounding No.

On a number of levels, and quite unexpectedly, Mexico welcomed me with open arms. I already had been "adopted" by two families here, one in the town in which I eventually settled and one in Mexico City. When I needed an operation in 2009, one of those families—an hour away from the hospital—showed up there in force, and some of them even slept in my room overnight, in case I should need anything. (In the United States, I could have died in my condominium and wouldn't have been discovered until the monthly mortgage payment was past due—and this is literally true.) My insurance agent, Olivia, showed up as well, to guide me through the intake process; and unlike the "Sicko" arrangements of health care in the United States, the company paid for something like 90% of the costs, without making me fight with them over the legitimacy of the claim. (I actually have a poem about her in my book *Counting Blessings;* can you imagine writing an affectionate poem about your health insurance agent in

FIELDS BOOK STORE

1419 POLK STREET
SAN FRANCISCO 94109
PHONE 673-2027

BOOKS NEW AND OLD

Oriental Philosophy
Psychology
Metaphysics - Astrology
Hermetics - Kabbalah
Sufi - Gurdjieff - Art
Tarot

10 | WHEEL of FORTUNE

Goethe's Faust

Wuthering Heights

the United States, or your HMO? "O mighty corporation, with tentacles flung wide...") In 2008, I was sought out by a major university in Mexico City, the Tecnológico de Monterrey, to join the faculty as a visiting professor, which I did for a year and a half; and discovered that instead of the bored "entertain me" attitude of American students, their Mexican counterparts were (for the most part) eager to learn. And soon after my arrival I was approached by several high-quality publications to write articles for them, in two cases on a regular basis. This eventually led to official status within Mexico as a writer-journalist, and to the publication of this collection of essays in Spanish translation, whereas no American publisher was even mildly interested. Indeed, most rejected it without even looking at it. This is a kind of censorship, to be sure, but not really one of an ideological nature. As a few agents and publishers were willing to tell me explicitly, American publishing has changed drastically since 2006, when I published my previous book. If 97% of it was about money prior to that date, the figure is now 100%, and clearly, a book like this is not going to make anybody rich. Hence the irony of the whole thing: if America were *not* the nation accurately described by Adlai Stevenson, there would be no need to write this book; but since it *is* a vapid, commercial, one-dimensional culture, the likelihood of this material making it into the public eye is virtually nil. I am, as a result, grateful to Amazon for making this self-publishing service available, although how many people will actually read these pages is an open question. It does, in short, come down to a question of values, and the American value-system (such as it is) should not be a mystery to anybody.

Only about half the articles in this collection, however, deal with the United States. Questions of value obviously extend beyond the boundaries of any one country; they are also larger than the realm of politics. Hence, I struggle here with issues of what constitutes progress, what the future seems to hold, how we know the inner and outer worlds, and what is finally important in human life. I am guessing that these are things the reader has also been thinking about, and hope that my own thoughts on these subjects might, as a result, be of some interest to at least a tiny minority.

A few acknowledgments are in order, before I sign off. I am grateful to Eduardo Rabasa, my editor at Sexto Piso Editorial, for his encouragement, support, and friendship over the years; Gustavo Vázquez, the editor of *Parteaguas*, for making me his "columnista internacional"; Alejandro Palma, a dear friend both insightful and erudite, whose feedback did much to stimulate my thinking; and Nomi Prins and Joseph Dispenza, who understood what I was up against, and provided a lot of moral support. I thank you, amigos; all of this has meant a great deal.

M.B.
Mexico
2010

PART I
LAMENT FOR
AMERICA

1. To See Ourselves as We Are Seen

I recall, shortly after the attacks of 9/11, a radio program in the United States that asked for brief statements on the part of journalists and editors from around the world as to how they viewed the events of that day. Most of the respondents, as might be expected, condemned the terrorists for the slaughter of innocents; and rightly so. But I was particularly struck by the response of the editor of some Pakistani newspaper–the name escapes me now–who added to the general condemnation something rather unexpected: "It is important for America to understand the impact it has on the rest of the world," he told his American audience. "Too often, it fails to take that into account in trying to assess the reactions of other nations to it." Of course, his exhortation was completely ignored in the United States; to this day, the vast majority of Americans believe that the attacks of 9/11 emerged from a political vacuum, being nothing more than the actions of men who were "insane" or "evil". U.S. foreign policy, apparently, had no part to play in these events.

The next Pakistani comment I came across regarding the events of that day was several years later, and of a very different order. *The Reluctant Fundamentalist*, by the Pakistani writer Mohsin Hamid, can be seen as a pointed fleshing-out of that editor's remarks. It won't have any more success in waking up the American people than did that immediate post-9/11 commentary, but the brilliance of this novel certainly makes it worth the effort. Indeed, I was hooked from the opening paragraph, and read the book in one sitting. Written in the form of a monologue delivered, at a café in Lahore, to an American CIA-type (or so it seems) by "Changez," the narrator, Hamid's prose has a limpid, natural quality that is both understated and seductive at the same time. Changez tells his silent listener the story of his life to date: as a bright Pakistani student, he won a scholarship to Princeton University, graduated with honors, and went on to a job as an analyst at a prestigious New York-based corporation, "Underwood Samson & Company". USC is in the business of "valuation," i.e., estimating the value of a company that another company might want to buy, or of a division of a company that the larger firm might want to liquidate. More often than not, the lives of workers are destroyed by the valuation. In one case, that of a publishing firm in Valparaiso, Chile, the intended goal is to eliminate the trade books section that deals in quality literature, so that the press can market books that have purely commercial value.

In the beginning, Changez is dazzled by his high-paying job, elegant Manhattan apartment, and the prestige derived from moving in corporate circles. He follows the company's directive to "focus on the fundamentals," i.e., the cash value of things. The social and political context in which his work is situated is not something that concerns him. All of this, however, starts to change after the attacks of 9/11, the American response to them, and the subsequent invasion of Afghanistan, a Muslim nation that borders his homeland. Ineluctably, Changez is led to grasp the nature of American society as a whole, and in particular, of the American empire. He sees how class-based and xenophobic the society is; how civilian deaths in countries under American attack are regarded as nothing more than "collateral damage"; and how "no country inflicts death so readily upon the inhabitants of other countries, [or] frightens so many people so far away, as America."

The real turning point comes during his work with the publishing house in Valparaiso. The elderly company chief, Juan-Bautista, reminds him of his maternal grandfather, with whom he was close. Juan-Bautista asks Changez what he knows of books, and the latter finds himself saying that his grand-uncle was a poet, and that books were loved in his family. The problem is that USC's goal is to evaluate the firm from a strictly financial viewpoint; it couldn't care less about the world of learning. Sensing Changez's internal conflict, Juan-Bautista takes him to dinner, and talks to him about the Janissaries, Christian boys captured by the Ottomans and trained to destroy their own civilization, until "they had nothing else to turn to". Changez gets the point: he himself is a modern-day Janissary, having sided with an empire that thinks nothing of ruining the life of someone like Juan-Bautista for the sake of monetary gain. It becomes impossible for him to keep pretending that his "valuations" are neutral. He finally betrays USC to save the deeper values he was raised with, and which he had never really given up. For Changez sees that the American Dream is not only shallow and illusory, but actually destructive of the deeper values of civilization; and even worse, is by now grounded in violence. Having lost his job and his visa, now back in Lahore, he tells his American audience of one:

> As a society, you were unwilling to reflect upon the shared pain that united you with those who attacked you. You retreated into myths of your own difference, assumptions of your own superiority. And you acted out these beliefs on the stage of the world, so that the entire planet was rocked by the repercussions of your tantrums, not least my family, now facing war thousands of miles away. Such an America had to be stopped in the interests not only of the rest of humanity, but also in your own.

Changez finally leaves the United States and becomes a university lecturer in Pakistan, popular for pulling no punches in his analysis of the American attempt to dominate the world. Eventually, as the title of the book seems to suggest, he is led to act on his beliefs in more radical ways.

With the exception of this final development, which gives the novel its concluding (and ambiguous) twist, it is difficult not to regard the story as autobiographical. Hamid himself is a Pakistani who grew up in Lahore, and subsequently studied at Princeton and Harvard. Although the prose is smooth and low-key, his passion over what the United States is doing in and to the world can hardly be disguised; and there is much here for Americans to learn, if they could only see themselves as others see them. For there is a definite relationship between macrocosm and microcosm: as the U.S. government behaves, so do its citizens, and this is hardly an accident. On a holiday with some Americans in Greece, for example, the narrator says that he found himself "wondering by what quirk of human history my companions—many of whom I would have regarded as upstarts in my own country, so devoid of refinement were they—were in a position to conduct themselves in the world as though they were its ruling class." Good question, and hardly irrelevant to American imperial designs and U.S. foreign policy since the end of World War II. Speaking again of the aftermath of 9/11, Changez relates to his listener how New York was suddenly soaking in American flags—on windshields, fluttering from buildings, even stuck on toothpicks: "They all seemed to proclaim: *We are America…the mightiest civilization the world has ever known; you have slighted us; beware our wrath.*"

That was indeed the mood, all right, and Hamid's lines remind me of that classic poem by Percy Shelley, "Ozymandias," in which a traveler in the desert finds the remains of a statue, now reduced to a pedestal, which bears the following words:

> My name is Ozymandias, king of kings:
> Look on my works, ye Mighty, and despair!

The traveler looks around, and all he can see is an empty landscape of sand stretching to infinity.

Everything passes; what else is there to say?

2. conspiracy vs. Conspiracy in American History

The notion that the parliamentary democracy of the industrial nations is a sham, and that the real power lies not in the hands of the people (or their elected representatives) but in the hands of a small, ruling elite is a view most closely associated with Karl Marx. This is one meaning of the word "conspiracy": the ruling class knows what its interests are, and it acts to protect them. In this sense of the term, conspiracy is equivalent to elite theory, because the implication is that the ruling class acts with a unified consciousness. Indeed, Marx argued that the emergence of serious conflicts within the ranks of the elite was a sign that the system was ripe for revolutionary overthrow.

Elite theory, then, holds that the people (or masses) are under the illusion that through their vote they control the direction of the ship of state, whereas the real captains of the ship—the heads of industry, the *eminences grises*—are not themselves on the ballot. The public does not get to vote for *them*, but rather for their paid representatives. Thus the post-election euphoria in the United States over Barack Obama was nothing more than a bubble, an illusion, because the lion's share of the $750 million he collected in campaign contributions (according to the Australian journalist John Pilger) came from Goldman Sachs, UBS AG, Lehman Brothers, J.P. Morgan Chase, Citigroup, Morgan Stanley, Credit Suisse, and the huge hedge fund Citadel Investment Group. These corporations, as we have come to understand, do not exactly have the welfare of the American people as their top priority; and it is also the case that having invested in a president, they expected a return on that investment once he took office. And as we know, they got it—as we saw in the financial bailout following the crash of 2008. It is for this reason that what we have in the United States, according to Harvard political scientist Michael Sandel, is a "procedural democracy": the form, the appearance, is democratic, but the actual content, the result, is not. As the eminent sociologist C. Wright Mills put it in 1956,

> In so far as the structural clue to the power elite today lies in the political order, that clue is the decline of politics as genuine and public debate of alternative decisions....America is now in considerable part more a formal political democracy than a democratic social structure, and even the formal political mechanics are weak.

While it is undoubtedly true that elites occasionally act in a deliberate and concerted way, it was Mills in particular who pointed out that the reality was significantly more nuanced than this. For the most part, it is not that the rich or super-rich get together in some corporate boardroom and ask themselves, "Now how can we best screw the workers and the middle class?" No, said Mills, what in fact happens is that they socialize together, in an informal sort of way, and recognize their class affiliations:

> Members of the several higher circles know one another as personal friends and even as neighbors; they mingle with one another on the golf course, in the gentlemen's clubs, at resorts, on transcontinen-

tal airplanes, and on ocean liners. They meet at the estates of mutual friends, face each other in front of the TV camera, or serve on the same philanthropic committee; and many are sure to cross one another's path in the columns of newspapers, if not in the exact cafés from which many of these columns originate....The conception of the power elite, accordingly, does *not* rest upon the assumption that American history since the origins of World War II must be understood as a secret plot, or as a great and co-ordinated conspiracy of the members of this elite. The conception rests upon quite impersonal grounds.

We are not, in short, talking about some sort of organized brotherhood, some quasi-Masonic financial clique, as it were. However—and this is the crucial point—in terms of concrete outcome, we might as well be. Mills goes on:

But, once the conjunction of structural trends and of the personal will to utilize it gave rise to the power elite, then plans and programs did occur to its members and indeed it is not possible to interpret many events and official policies...without reference to the power elite.

Mills' work falls more into the category of social criticism than of social science per se; he was not big on facts and figures. But in the fifty-plus years since he wrote the above words, his profile of American democracy as illusory has been fleshed out by numerous sociologists and political scientists armed with reams of data. Thus a recent work in this genre, *Superclass*, by David Rothkopf, identifies a global elite of roughly 6,000 individuals who are running the show, worldwide, and the top fifty financial institutions that control nearly $50 trillion in assets. Plot or no plot, the results are the same.

This, then, is elite theory, or what I call conspiracy with a small "c". And it is a real fact of American political life, no question about it. But what may be even more significant than this are what I call Conspiracies with a capital "C", by which I mean the unconscious mythologies, or isms, that govern that life. This was the thing that Marx, and Mills, both missed (though the Italian sociologist Antonio Gramsci did come close to it with his notion of "hegemony," or the symbolic control of society): the elites aren't doing anything that the masses don't already agree with; which is why, certainly, in the United States, socialism never really had a chance. When Henry Wriston, who was president of the Council on Foreign Relations during 1951-64, wrote that U.S. foreign policy "is the expression of the will of the people," he knew what he was talking about. As many observers (even American ones) have pointed out, what the American people–less than 5% of the world's population–want is an indulgent and wasteful lifestyle, in which they consume 25% of the world's energy. Thus in the presidential debates of October 2008, Barack Obama referred to the 25% figure, and then talked about ways of ensuring that that rate of consumption continue unchecked. He did not, as did Jimmy Carter more than thirty years ago, argue that growth was not necessarily a positive thing, that Americans needed to burn less energy, and that the American military–the guarantor of that profligate lifestyle—had to be scaled down accordingly. Indeed, within two years of taking office, Mr. Carter was popularly regarded as something of a joke, and by 1980 Ronald Reagan, who told the American people they could have it all, was elected by a landslide. So while it is true that elites run the show, they nevertheless govern with the (manufactured) consent of the people. As the nineteenth-century Sioux holy man, Chief Sitting Bull, was supposed to have said, "possessions are a disease with them." But his was hardly the majority view—not then, not now.

What, then, are the major Conspiracies, or isms, of American life? I think we can identify four in particular.

1. The notion of Americans as the "chosen people," and of the nation as a "City on a Hill." This latter phrase—quoted by both Barack Obama and Sarah Palin in the 2008 presidential campaign—goes back to the future governor of the Massachusetts Bay Colony, John Winthrop, as he was sailing from England to America on the *Arabella* in 1630: "We shall find that the God of Israel is among us....He shall make us a praise and glory....For we must Consider that we shall be as a City upon a Hill. The eyes of all people are upon us."

The idea is that it would be America's unique mission to bring democracy to all the peoples of the earth, inasmuch as the American way of life was (obviously) the best. (Iraq is merely the latest manifestation of this way of thinking.) In fact, the Puritans took the Jews of the Old Testament as their model, in which the exodus from Egypt, and invasion of Canaan, were regarded as the paradigm for the establishment of the Colonies. The notion that the story of the United States is the primary manifestation of God's will on earth has an enormous hold on the American psyche. "American exceptionalism," Alexis de Tocqueville called it; it is with us to this day.

2. Along with this we have Ism No. 2: the existence, in the United States, of a "civil religion." This was first pointed out by the sociologist Robert Bellah in 1967, the fact that despite the presence of Catholicism, Judaism, and numerous Protestant sects in America, the real religion of the American people was America itself. To be an American is regarded (unconsciously, by Americans) as an ideological/religious commitment, not an accident of birth. This is why critics of the United States are immediately labeled "un-American," and are practically regarded as traitors. (Quite ridiculous, when you think about it: can you imagine a Swedish critic of Sweden, for example, being attacked as "un-Swedish"?) The historian Sidney Mead pegged it correctly when he called America "the nation with the soul of a church," while another historian, Richard Hofstadter, declared that "It has been our fate as a nation not to have ideologies, but to be one." Quite obviously, this is not a position that encourages self-reflection.

3. The third unconscious mythology is the one identified by Frederick Jackson Turner in 1893: the existence of a supposedly endless frontier, into which the American people would expand geographically. Eventually, it became an economic frontier, and finally an imperial one–Manifest Destiny gone global. This lay at the heart of the Carter-Reagan debate, for the notion of limits to growth is almost

a form of heresy in an American context. The American Dream envisions a world without limits, in which the goal, as the gangster (played by Edward G. Robinson) tells Humphrey Bogart in *Key Largo*, is simply "more". De Tocqueville had already, in the 1830s, commented on the great "restlessness" of the American people; and more than a century later, the British journalist Alistair Cooke remarked that what were regarded as luxuries throughout most of the world, were regarded as necessities in the United States. If Americans never had much of an interest in socialism, they probably had even less interest in Buddhism, the occasional Zen center notwithstanding. It was not for nothing that the historian William Leach entitled his study of late-nineteenth-century American expansionism, *Land of Desire*.

4. Finally, we have a national character based on extreme individualism–Emerson's "Self-Reliance." As the historian Joyce Appleby describes it, this originated in the shift in the definition of the word "virtue" that took place in the Colonies in the 1790s. Previous to that time, the word had a European (or even classical) definition, namely "the capacity of some men to rise above private interests and devote themselves to the public good." By 1800, the definition had undergone a complete inversion: "virtue" now meant the capacity to look out for oneself in an opportunistic environment. Whereas the former definition was adhered to by the Federalists, the Jeffersonian Republicans actively promoted the latter definition, as part of the new nation's break with England and all things European. Life was not to be about service to the community, but

rather about competition and the acquisition of goods. This is summarized in the popular American expression, "There is no free lunch." The "self-made man" is expected to make it on his own.

There have been very few dissenters to this fourth ism; in many ways, American history can be seen as the story of a nation consistently choosing individual solutions over collective ones. One American who did dissent, however, was Bill Wilson, the founder of Alcoholics Anonymous. In *Twelve Steps and Twelve Traditions* he wrote: "The philosophy of self-sufficiency is not paying off. Plainly enough, it is a bone-crushing juggernaut whose final achievement is ruin."

And "ruin" is the operative word here. While there is certainly an upside to these four isms–the sunny face of technological innovation and the Yankee "can-do" mentality, for example–in the long run these unconscious mythologies, in dialectical fashion, began to turn against those caught up in their magic spell. It surely cannot be an accident that 25% of all the world's prisoners are incarcerated in American jails (1% of the entire U.S. adult population); that two-thirds of the global antidepressant market is accounted for by the United States; that 24% of the American population say that it's OK to use violence in the pursuit of one's goals, 44% support the torture of suspected terrorists, and 39% want Muslims in the United States to be required to carry a religious ID on them at all times (why not just make it a yellow star, and be done with it?); that the country has one of the highest percentages of single-person dwellings in the world (27.5%)), the world's highest overall crime rate, a homicide rate that is four times that of France and the U.K., the largest military budget (by several orders of magnitude), and the greatest number of shopping malls of any country on the planet. The data on ignorance, which I have documented elsewhere, are breathtaking, and Robert Putnam's description (in *Bowling Alone*) of the collapse of community, trust, and friendship is one of the saddest things I have ever read. Dialectically, and ironically, American "success" became American ruin; the crash of October 2008 was merely the tip of the iceberg.

The power of isms, certainly in the American case, derives from the fact that they are unconscious, embedded deep in the psyche. They constitute Conspiracies in that those who hold them are like marionettes on strings, screaming "Obama!" (for example) without realizing that the new president can no more buck the elites running the country than he can dismantle the mythologies that drive its citizens—himself included. As for the individual, so for the nation: the only hope is to see ourselves as we are seen, from the outside, as it were. And therein lies the paradox. For the four Conspiracies close in on themselves, forming a kind of mirror-lined glass sphere that does not permit any dissonant information to enter. Sandel, Mills, Rothkopf, Bellah, Mead, Leach, Appleby, Putnam—America's finest, really—will never become household words, and if they did, it would probably be as objects of contempt. For this is finally the most terrifying thing about isms or Conspiracies: we do not choose them; rather, it is they that choose us.

References

"Anti-Muslim Sentiments Fairly Commonplace," http://media.gallup.com/WorldPoll/PDF/AntiMuslim-Sentiment81006.pdf, 10 August 2006

Joyce Appleby, *Capitalism and a New Social Order* (New York: New York University Press, 1984).

Charles Barber, *Comfortably Numb* (New York: Pantheon, 2008). The 66% figure for the American share of the world antidepressant market, however, is based on dollar sales, and U.S. prices for prescription medications are typically higher than they are in other countries. Hence, the actual figure for consumption of these medications, on a comparative worldwide basis, is unclear; although we can reasonably expect that the United States would be pretty high up on the charts.

Robert Bellah, "Civil Religion in America," *Daedalus*, No. 96 (1967), pp. 1-21.

Morris Berman, *Dark Ages America* (New York: W.W. Norton, 2006).

Christie Findlay, "Loneliness: More Than Just a Bad Mood," *AARP Bulletin Today*, 9 April 2009, http://bulletin.aarp.org/opinions/othervoices/articles/loneliness_more_than_just_a_bad_mood.html.

http://wiki.answers.com/Q/What_country_have_ the_most_number_of_shopping_malls.

Nick Juliano, "Poll: 44% of Americans favor torture for terrorist suspects,"
http://www.liveleak.com/view?i=05f_1214377613.

Jill Lepore, "Rap Sheet," *The New Yorker*, 9 November 2009, pp. 79-83.

Cathie Madsen, "Crime Rates Around the World," December 2006, http://www.nationmaster.com/article/ Crime-Rates-Around-the-World. "Overall crimes" refers to burglary, homicide, rape, and robbery. As far as homicide goes, America is No. 1 if nations with severe political turmoil are not included (if they are, then Colombia is No. 1).

C. Wright Mills, *The Power Elite* (New York: Oxford University Press, 1956).

Jacqueline Olds and Richard Schwartz, *The Lonely American* (Boston: Beacon Press, 2009).

John Pilger, "After Bobby Kennedy," *New Statesman*, 29 May 2008.

"Record Number of Americans in Jail," *San Francisco Sentinel*, 18 October 2009, p. 1 (data compiled from Justice Department and Census Bureau statistics), www.sanfranciscosentinel.com/?p=19911.

Jeremy Rifkin, *The European Dream* (New York: Jeremy P. Tarcher/Penguin, 2004).

Michael Sandel, *Democracy's Discontent* (Cambridge, MA: Belknap Press, 1996).

Frederick Jackson Turner, "The Significance of the Frontier in American History," lecture to the American Historical Association, Chicago, 1893; reprinted in numerous anthologies and available at www.historians.org/pubs/archives/Turnerthesis.htm.

Donald White, *The American Century* (New Haven: Yale University Press, 1996).

3. Rope-a-Dope: The Chump Factor in U.S. Foreign Policy

It should be clear by now that the four "Conspiracies" outlined above have an enormous hold on the American psyche. This in turn has led to a kind of national blindness in U.S. foreign policy. In particular, they set Americans up to be chumps, and most nations of the world learned long ago that the way to deal with Washington is simply to tell it what it wants to hear. "Though Americans rarely discuss their national tendency to credulousness," writes the Irish journalist Eamonn Fingleton, "it is a fact of life that is well understood by tricksters and con men around the world." This holds true even for America's Anglo-Saxon allies, such as Great Britain and the Commonwealth nations, for whom the naïveté of Americans is legendary. We can expect, then, that it would be even truer for the countries of East Asia, as Fingleton describes it in his illuminating book, *In the Jaws of the Dragon.*

As a prime example of this, Fingleton recounts the story of postwar Japan. Gen. Douglas MacArthur, head of the occupying forces there, sought to "Americanize" the Japanese, get them to embrace Western capitalism and democracy. That he succeeded remains, to this day, part of the U.S. national mythology. In MacArthur's view, democracy was irresistible, and one year after his arrival he spoke of a "spiritual revolution" that "ensued almost overnight," reversing 2,000 years of Japanese tradition. "This revolution of the spirit among the Japanese people represents no thin veneer to serve the purposes of the present," he proudly declared.

But of course, a thin veneer was exactly what it represented. What MacArthur failed to grasp was that a few months' contact with friendly American GI's was not enough to bring about such a cultural miracle. In fact, the Japanese were very clever in deflecting MacArthur's attempts to impose American values upon them, and they were able to do this because they understood that he was a chump. They recognized quite quickly that he was vain and self-absorbed, so they treated him like an emperor—which worked like a charm. A similar type of flattery was also effective with other top U.S. officials stationed in Japan. These men were completely ignorant of this very old civilization, of its history and its psychology, and yet saw themselves as capable of miraculously transforming it. After all, how could the Japanese not want to be Americans? To this day Americans believe that it is only a matter of time before non-Western nations come around to American values.*

The problem was that the Americans had to work through Japanese officials to bring about the reforms they sought. These officials rarely said no, but were adept at scuttling any such initiatives. The expression for this in Japanese is *menju fukuhai*—to cooperate with the face, but disobey with the belly. Hence the Japanese worked hard to make relations with the Americans as smooth as possible, on the surface, and cooperated with them on many unimportant issues. But behind the smiles was a deep bitterness over the dropping of atomic bombs on Hiroshima and Nagasaki, which caused the grisly deaths of hundreds of thousands of civilians.

It proved easy to play the Americans for fools. Right under MacArthur's nose, the Japanese created a cosmetic, democratic persona, writes Fingleton, a pseudo-democracy that was presented to outsiders as the real thing. Meanwhile, Japan's elite bureaucrats quietly arranged sweeping powers for themselves, enabling them to rule from behind the scenes. The reality of postwar Japan, even allowing for extensive Westernization, has been a semi-authoritarian society with a nationalist agenda, not a genuine American-style democracy. So while the Americans saw postwar Japan as a showcase of capitalism, the truth is that it had decidedly noncapitalist features, such as a system of lifetime employment and a government-controlled banking industry. Contrary to MacArthur's claim, it was very much a "thin veneer to serve the purposes of the present."

And of the future as well. The fact is that the Japanese were in it for the long haul, and now, as creditors to a debtor nation, they underwrite a wasteful and self-indulgent lifestyle that they could cripple quite severely, if they chose to do so. Indeed, by the end of 2008 Japan was the major purchaser of U.S. Treasury bills, to the tune of nearly 1.2 trillion dollars.**

If Japan managed to exploit the chump factor in American foreign policy quite brilliantly, China can be said to have elevated this technique to an art. Fingleton points out that the belief in Washington (following the mythology of universal democracy) has been, for many years now, that as China prospers it will become more democratic. China lets the United States believe whatever it wants, but the truth is just the opposite: China is getting rich *because* it is authoritarian, *because* it is opposed to Western values and to the notion of a laissez-faire market economy. The Chinese economic system is rather one of state capitalism run by iron bureaucratic control, and involving a labyrinthine system of trade barriers, an artificially undervalued currency, and widespread institutionalized bribery–a "shark tank," as one China-watcher has called it. Writing in *Newsweek* magazine (19 January 2009), Rana Foroohar says that this is a place "where the state doctors statistics, manipulates the stock markets, fixes prices in key industries, owns many strategic industries outright, and staffs key bank posts with Communist Party members." While pundits such as Thomas Friedman and Francis Fukuyama assure us that Western logic is universal and will eventually sweep the world, and the *Wall Street Journal* proclaims that the Asian nations are "racing to build an American-style consumer economy," the Chinese use this kind of American self-deception as a cover for their own non-Western agenda. For Chinese society follows a very different set of rules, ones partly derived from Confucius, in which ideology counts for nothing and results count for everything. In this system, the end justifies the means all the time; "truth" is not a matter of great concern. In the Confucian scheme of things, the "truth" is merely contextual–you just say what is appropriate in the circumstances, not what actually is the case. This is what, from a Western point of view, would be called amoral, but the Chinese see it as simply pragmatic. Deng Xiaoping, who was the de facto leader of the People's Republic of China from 1978 to the early 1990s, captured the attitude succinctly when he remarked, "It doesn't matter if a cat is white or black, as long as it catches the mouse." As for the masses, they are expected to exhibit obedience, loyalty, and self-sacrifice; nothing more. The key concept is "harmony"–the core value of Japanese society as well.

Western observers such as Friedman are regarded by the Chinese as preachy fools–like MacArthur, deeply self-absorbed and easily taken in by phony praise for writing the approved Chinese version of things. China will, for example, display a token openness, such as allowing Coca-Cola and McDonald's to set up shop there; but it is finally just PR, not something that alters the rules of the game in any substantive way. "Playing" the United States includes, for example, promising to open up the Chinese market to American companies...but then it turns out that there is a forest of red tape designed to slow the process down. In 2006, for example, foreign banks in China were restricted to narrow activities such as processing foreign currency loans and deposits. Fingleton points out that since the United States has always been convinced that the triumph of free-market ideology is just around the corner, it has, for decades, been a chump for a one-way free trade policy with the Confucian world. While China's trade surplus with America was $10.4 billion in 1990, fifteen years later it was up to $202 billion–the largest trade imbalance between any two nations in history. According to *Le Monde diplomatique* (November 2008), China holds 922 billion dollars' worth of U.S. Treasury bills, and is sitting on the world's largest dollar reserves—almost two trillion.

There are a few economists who, like Fingleton, see all this as deliberately planned. In the past decade China invested more than one trillion dollars in U.S. government bonds and government-backed mortgage debt, which served to lower interest rates and fuel the consumption binge in the United States. But clearly, borrowing from abroad for a consumption orgy at home is a formula for economic disaster; only a nation fogged over by The American Way of Life could fail to see that. Writing in the *International Herald Tribune* (27-28 December 2008), Mark Landler points out that the United States continues to be addicted to foreign creditors. Huge amounts of money will be needed to fund President Obama's stimulus package, and the country will need China to keep buying that debt, thereby perpetuating the American habit of dependency and egregious consumption. America is so heavily indebted to China, says Fingleton, that the situation already looks like the relationship between a colony and an imperial capital. The political fallout from such an arrangement should be obvious: analysts at the U.S. Naval War College calculate that China will be equal to the United States as a military power in the Asia-Pacific region by the year 2020.

"To subdue the enemy without fighting is the acme of skill," wrote the Chinese military commander Sun Tzu, in the sixth century B.C. Around the same time, the Athenian statesman Solon was urging his audiences to "know thyself." If America had managed to do the latter, it might not now be falling victim to the former.

*However, Fingleton also believes that MacArthur was aware of the charade, but went along with it because he aspired to be the Republican candidate for president in the 1948 election. If true, this would lend a somewhat different interpretation to the events of post-war Japan, although the results would be the same.

**Two years later, Japan continues to be a major holder of T-bills, although the figure cited here may be dated given the severe economic downturn that hit Japan in the wake of the crash of 2008.

4. How to Get Out of Iraq

In the spring of 2006 I received an invitation to attend the launching of the Washington, D.C. branch of the Independent Institute, a think tank based in Oakland, California. Attendance, it noted, was by invitation only, and there would be five prominent speakers, who would be discussing ways of getting the United States out of Iraq. I didn't know that much about the Independent Institute, save that it counted among its directors Ivan Eland, who had written what was to my mind an incisive analysis of American imperial history, *The Empire Has No Clothes.* That I got invited at all was something I never quite figured out, but why quarrel with the gods, I thought. I put on a suit and tie and took the Metro downtown.

The event was on a weekend afternoon, if I remember correctly. It was, indeed, a select audience, because the symposium was held in a room with a seating capacity of at most sixty or seventy people. C-SPAN was there to film it for its "BookTV" series; Daniel Ellsberg, who lives in California, came in for the event. Speakers included Ivan Eland, Gen. William Odum (retired), historian-journalist Gareth Porter, and two others whose names escape me now. Somebody from the Independent Institute gave a brief introduction, and then the speakers launched into their talks.

What then unrolled was an object lesson in irony. Only about half the people in the audience bothered to listen to what was going on. Indeed, it seemed like every thirty seconds someone's cell phone went off, and the person would answer their phone, and then take the call, walking out of the room as they did so (at least they had the decency to leave, but then, this was a few years ago). This went on almost constantly. The woman seated to my left, about thirty years of age with a distinctly teenage kind of energy to her, paid no attention to any of the speakers; for the entire length of the conference, she sat there staring at her cell phone, text-messaging other people. It never occurred to any of these cell phone addicts—and I'm referring to at least thirty-five individuals—that inasmuch as they had been invited to a private event, the least they could do was to actually be present at it. That is to say, to turn off their phones and sit for the allotted hour or so and listen to what the speakers were saying. No: these people were so "important" that it was perfectly OK to them to ignore the entire meeting and respond to these "urgent" messages. (It's amazing how many messages become "urgent" when one has a cell phone.) To hell with everybody else, is the idea here; my personal life comes first.

Before we ask ourselves how the United States might get out of Iraq, we might ask ourselves how it got in there in the first place. And what immediately comes to mind, for me at least, is hubris. America, and America alone, will command the space, and the governments, of other nations, and tell them how they are going to think and live. A huge chunk of this nation—probably, the vast majority—regards this as a perfectly sensible and legitimate foreign policy. But suppose the shoe were on the other foot, and there were a nation in the world more powerful than us (which is, let's face it, only a matter of time), and it decided that it didn't like our government and our president, and would, as a result, institute a "regime change." So it bombed and invaded us, took us over, murdered several hundred thousand civilians, removed our leaders from power, and set up a government whose actions it would personally direct. This is completely acceptable to the American people when the United States is doing it to another nation; but these very same people would (rightly) react with horrified indignation if another nation would attempt to do anything even vaguely similar to us. Hubris means I Come First, I'll Do What I Want, I'll act however I want in your space, and if you don't like it, too bad for you.

This issue of space is an important one. Western cultures believe, following Euclid and Newton, that all space is functionally equivalent: just one big box, so to speak. But as other cultures know, this is demonstrably incorrect: the space of a subway car, or a university classroom, or a church, for example, are qualitatively very different, sequentially demonstrating an increasing amount of coherence and purpose. (We are in fact aware of this when we speak of the ambience of a restaurant, as restaurant reviews often do. All spaces are *not* equivalent, quite obviously.) Pure Newtonian space has no inherent meaning, and in that sense one might as well impose one's will on it, for it is merely a receptacle. But sacred space–to take the other extreme–is soaking in meaning, and acting in a highly individualistic manner in such a context would not be appropriate. The space of a symposium or conference is somewhere in between, like a university classroom; but it surely has enough meaning imbued in it that to take it over for one's own purposes would be to do violence to it, in effect. To show the space respect is to play by its rules, not your own. But just the reverse was happening in the space of this gathering in downtown Washington, and this raises the question of the *mental* space of the participants—their values (conscious or unconscious) and way of conducting themselves.

In effect, the problem of the United States in Iraq showed up, in microcosm, in the behavior of much of the audience at the Independent Institute's symposium on how to get out of Iraq. When you think about it, this behavior was, socially speaking, idiotic (in ancient Greece, an "idiot" was a person who did not know how to relate to the larger society), and what these attendees were doing amounted to a form of social violence. They came to a symposium on how to get out of Iraq, and then on an individual level displayed the identical attitude of the American government toward Iraq: I Come First, I'll Do What I Want, I'll act however I want in your space, and if you don't like it, too bad for you. I'm guessing that almost all of the audience was opposed to American imperial policy in the Middle East; but if your psyche is ultimately the same as that of the president's in terms of one's individual right to the space of others, what difference does it make?

The truth is that macro-aggression is not really possible without a cultural basis of micro-aggression. For America to stop being an imperial power, arrogantly imposing (or attempting to impose) its will on the rest of the world, its individual citizens have to stop being mini-imperialists; they would have to respect the space of other people. But this is not very likely to happen, because it– i.e., nonrespect, in the form of extreme individualism–is the very fabric of American social life, and thus, in effect, invisible. This conforms very well to Marshall McLuhan's famous quip, that the last thing a fish is aware of in its environment is water. Thus for me to have suggested to the woman on my left, for example, that coming to the symposium only to do e-mail for the entire length of the conference was rude, would have left her not only enraged, but genuinely bewildered: What could I possibly mean by that, since "surely" she has every right to do whatever she wants, regardless of the context. Obviously, if everybody's behavior is narcissistic and arrogant, then narcissism and arrogance become "normal".*

Of course, rude and arrogant cell phone use is now a near-universal phenomenon; it is no longer restricted to the United States. This is because for many countries, America and globalization are "hip," the wave of the future, and so imitation of this behavior is very hard to resist. The fact is that you don't get technology "for free," as it were; the world view or mindset of the context in which it emerges comes along with the hardware. As McLuhan, Marcuse, and a number of other philosophers have demonstrated, technology is never value-neutral; imported into culture B from culture A, it "infects" the value-system of culture B with the value-system of culture A. I personally witnessed such a change in Barcelona over the period 2004-5, during which time cell phone use-ratio went from one out of a hundred persons to one out of three. As a result, the place went from a quiet and charming European city to a noisy, commercial, American one in the space of a year. Narcissistic and imperious behavior, in other words, becomes a kind of norm, with literally nobody noticing it.**

In any case, there we all were, at a symposium to explore how to stop being imperialists, when the cause of it all was literally right under our noses. (As one sociologist famously remarked, "There is more sociology in a department of sociology than there is in the rest of the world.") Instead of discussing military strategy, Shiites vs. Sunnis, the geopolitics of the Middle East, etc. etc., we might have done better to have turned the analytical lens back onto ourselves, and just observed what "normal" American behavior amounts to. Then the path to getting out of Iraq, and to not creating future Iraqs, no longer seems obscure: the United States will stop being the United States when Americans stop being Americans. What are the chances, do you think?

*In *The Lonely American* (Boston: Beacon Press, 2009), Jacqueline Olds and Richard Schwartz point out that the very triviality of such examples highlights their importance, because over time, they add up. It's the small, everyday choices people make about how they use technology that has a cumulative effect. "Little" decisions such as whether to interrupt a conversation with a friend in order to take a cell phone call–very rude behavior, when you think about it–"are powerful," they write, "because they are cumulative and because they fuel a vicious cycle," namely the cycle of distancing, of disengagement (not to mention, of demonstrating one's "importance"). The connection between this and Iraq is not as far-fetched as it might initially appear.

**For more on Barcelona, see my online article, "A Tale of Two Cultures: A London-Barcelona Diary," *Logos*, Vol. 4 No. 3 (Summer 2005), at http://www.logosjournal.com/issue_4.3/main.htm.

5. Locating the Enemy: Myth vs. Reality in U.S. Foreign Policy

Thematically speaking, there are many ways of looking at American history. In what follows, I want to examine one particular strand, perhaps an odd one for an historian, for it is as much spiritual or metaphysical as it is, say, social or political. The psychologist Ralph White, many years ago, described history as "psychology teaching by examples," and it is something of that nature that I would like to pursue in the following discussion.

The central point of the American Revolution was the rejection of England and the rest of Europe, the feudal world of hierarchy, privilege, and typically, religious intolerance. Ours would be an egalitarian society, in which the opportunity for advancement would be available to all (slaves, women, and Native Americans excepted, of course, but when their struggles came to pass, it was in the name of this principle). The Old World represented everything that the new one rejected, and thus the Republic based itself, from the very beginning, on the premise of the rejection of something else–what the German philosopher Hegel would later refer to as "negative identity." Negative identity is a phenomenon whereby you define yourself by what you are not. This has enormous advantages, especially in terms of the hardening of psychological boundaries and the fortification of the ego; one can mobilize a great deal of energy on this basis, and the new nation certainly did. In fact, 100 years after the signing of the Declaration of Independence, the United States was producing one-third of the entire world's manufactured goods–pretty impressive, as I'm sure the reader will agree. The down side, however, as Hegel noted, is that this way of generating an identity for yourself can never tell you who you actually *are*, in the affirmative sense. It leaves, in short, an emptiness at the center, such that you always have to be in opposition to something, or even at war with someone or something, in order to feel real.

The dynamics of identity by opposition leaves us with a cluster of questions we might ask of American history: How have Americans filled their inner void over the last 230 years (or more)? How genuinely threatening have the nations or ideologies been that we chose to oppose? And finally, what is the end product of all this opposition?

1. One of the most intriguing things about the United States is that genuinely alternative voices only very rarely get heard. Questions of a truly fundamental nature almost never seem to get asked, certainly not by the TV networks or the mainstream press. Consider the presidential debates of 2004. The two candidates certainly *seemed* to be at opposing ends of the political spectrum, and the media was definitely on board with this perception, portraying the choice as a stark one, involving two fundamentally different visions of America's future. Yet although Kerry and Bush were energetically duking it out for all to see, when push came to shove the foreign policy approaches of the two men were different in style, not in substance (something that was also true of the McCain-Obama debates of 2008); and in general, it was remarkable how little

of a fundamental nature got raised. No one–questioners included–used the words "empire" or "colonialism," or referred to the U.S.-backed Israeli occupation of Palestinian territory, or even mentioned Abu Ghraib or the Geneva Conventions. The choice was never put before the American people as to whether America ought to follow an imperial agenda or reject the same; nor was any mention made of faith-based "reality" vs. empirical evidence as appropriate criteria of truth. Kerry scrupulously avoided any reference to our close relationship to the repressive and corrupt regime of Saudi Arabia, or to the Project for the New American Century, which I'll discuss below–a group of neoconservatives who had been planning the war in Iraq as far back as 1990. Neither candidate talked about alternative energy sources, or the fact that we could not expect to have an indefinite supply of oil; and there was certainly no questioning of our "right" to keep burning 25% of the world's energy. Not much of a debate, when you get down to it.

Consider also the fact that the *New York Times*, typically regarded as the bastion of the so-called liberal establishment, actually led us *into* the Iraq war of 2003 by publishing dubious (i.e., largely unverified) front-page stories about weapons of mass destruction almost daily in the run-up to the war, as a number of scholars and news analysts, including the *Times*' own columnist, Frank Rich, subsequently demonstrated. In the lead-up to the war, the only major news magazine that was arguing that the whole thing was a charade–"pre-cooked," as Patrick Buchanan subsequently put it–was *The Nation*, whose circulation amounts to about 100,000 readers and is for the most part regarded as a "fringe" publication, if it is regarded at all.

The almost complete absence of skeptical pre-war reporting brings to mind the argument of sociologist Seymour Martin Lipset in *American Exceptionalism.* Lipset points out that in both the United States and Western Europe you are free to criticize the government or its policies, but it is only in the United States that you get branded as "un-American" for doing so, and your loyalty thrown open to question. A European critic, he notes, would never be labeled by his or her opponents as "un-Swedish" or "un-Italian," for example; but in the U.S., this smearing of dissenters is in pretty common, and it goes back a long way. "Those who complain of American life," wrote Ralph Waldo Emerson, "are not Americans." In other words, we *say* dissent is patriotic, that it is crucial to a democratic society, but this is largely lip service. When someone actually puts it into practice, tries to voice a critique of a fundamental nature, we label it disloyalty or treason, or just ignore them. The Vietnam years were a perfect example of this (the former especially), when crowds screamed "love it or leave it" at antiwar protesters–protesters who, in retrospect, proved to be completely correct in their accusation that the government was lying to the American people and actually had no idea of what it was doing in Southeast Asia.

Until recently, it never struck me that all of this was a religious reaction, which is what I'm really getting at here. I recall, in the spring of 2004, walking up Connecticut Avenue in Washington, D.C., with a friend of mine, a woman in her early thirties who worked as an editor for a scientific institute, and who was extremely bright. We were talking about the upcoming presidential election, and I said to her that given the nature of the Bush-Cheney administration, it would not surprise me if they were trying to figure out how to use the possibility of a terrorist attack to cancel or postpone that election; and I added that given the complete nonreaction of the American public to the recent revelations about Abu Ghraib, I doubted that the American electorate would care all that much. At this point she completely lost it, began screaming at me, in the street, that I was delusional, and that if I thought so little of the United States, why didn't I just leave the country. That was, I regret to say, the end of our friendship; I never heard from her again. (I also decided, two years later, to take her advice.) Of course, as the reader is probably aware, on July 19 of that year the international edition of *Newsweek* broke the story that the White House had, for several months, been discussing the possibility of suspending the election with the Department of Justice; and the reaction to that revelation was—as in the case of Abu Ghraib—complete silence. I thought of e-mailing the article to Sara, but I realized it was no use: what was at work here was a form of religion, and typically, reason is no match for it.

Much the same thing happened to me nearly two years later when I was interviewed by conservative radio stations on the occasion of the publication of my book *Dark Ages America*. In one case, when I mentioned that the war in Vietnam had cost us two-thirds of a trillion dollars in 1967 dollars, the talk show host began swearing at me on the air, yelling that we lost that war because of "the hippies and the commies." I paused for a moment, took a deep breath, and then told him that I knew of no major American historian who would agree with that assessment; whereupon my "interviewer" hung up the phone. As the historian Loren Baritz states in his sad and brilliant study of Vietnam (*Backfire*), "Myths do not yield to facts." Rather, he goes on, they lie "beneath the surface, more in the bloodstream than in the mind, in the national atmosphere rather than in specific policies." To be more anatomically exact, they are lodged in the limbic brain, not in the frontal lobes; but the metaphor here, of thinking by the blood, is a good one.

2. Perhaps we need to define the term "religion" a little more broadly. As already noted (Essay #2), the presence of what he termed a "civil religion" in America was the subject of an article by Robert Bellah, published more than forty years ago. The separation of church and state, wrote Bellah, has not denied the political realm a religious dimension, for the transcendent goal that America feels charged with is the obligation to carry out God's will on earth. Thus the Declaration of Independence contains four references to God, and religious expression permeates Washington's first inaugural address. The Founding Fathers talked a lot in these terms, but they were not referring to any particular religion, Christianity included. Rather, the American religion is that of fulfilling a mission, of bringing a new world into being. It is an activist

and moralistic religion, rather than an inward or contemplative one. For many Americans, the nation came to occupy a place in their lives that traditionally had been occupied by their church. This is why, while other nations have a sense of themselves derived from a common history, being an American is regarded as an ideological/religious commitment and not a matter of birth. "To be an American," wrote the philosopher George Santayana, "is of itself almost a moral condition." Hence, as I already indicated, those who reject American values are "un-American" by definition. "Americans," writes Seymour Martin Lipset,

> are utopian moralists who press hard to institutionalize virtue, to destroy evil people, and eliminate wicked institutions and practices. A majority even tell pollsters that God is the moral guiding force of American democracy. They tend to view social and political dramas as morality plays, as battles between God and the Devil, so that compromise is virtually unthinkable.

At the center of that religion, then, lies the notion that it is America's mission to democratize the rest of the world (by force if necessary); that we are, in effect, the primary agent of God's activity in history.

So that's the religion. What is its origin? The view of what they were doing, in coming to America, was taken by the Puritans from the bible, specifically from Exodus: a group of people, chosen by God, leave a corrupt and decadent society, cross a body of water, come into Canaan, subdue the land, and establish Israel, a land flowing with milk and honey. In the novel *White Jacket*, Herman Melville writes: "we Americans are the peculiar, chosen people–the Israel of our time; we bear the ark of the liberties of the world." All this goes back, as we have seen, to John Winthrop and his reference to America as a "City upon a Hill."

"In countless ways," writes Loren Baritz, "Americans know in their gut...that we have been Chosen to lead the world in public morality and to instruct it in political virtue." This means that those who disagree or oppose us are by definition enemies of virtue, and of God. That we are the *light*, and that it is our duty to bring that light to others, to the darkness, shows up, for example, in the speeches of Woodrow Wilson, in John Kennedy's inaugural address, and in Ronald Reagan's direct echo of Winthrop, that we were a City on a Hill, whereas the Soviet Union was the "evil empire." It means that we are compelled to intervene in the affairs of others; that we are, in the title of right-wing neoconservative writer Robt Kagan's latest book, a "Dangerous Nation." There is, in short, a One Right Way, and those who refuse to follow it are either wicked or stupid. Our mission, then, is to convert others to the truth as we understand it.

The leading scholar of the formation of the American identity is Harvard University's Sacvan Bercovitch, arguably the most influential Americanist of the last forty years. In *The Puritan Origins of the American Self*, Bercovitch documents the emergence, in the seventeenth century, of the American self as the incarnation of a universal providential plan. This, he argues, supplied the American craving for spiritual identity. The American, writes Bercovitch, "had to justify himself by justifying America." "To be an American is to assume a prophetic identity." We get some idea, then, of why criticism of America typically generates rage among the population at large: it means your whole psychological life is threatened.

The roots of America's prophetic identity run deep. Puritan texts of the seventeenth century constantly refer to the ancient Hebrew model, with titles such as *Passing Through the Red Sea*, or *Journey out of Aegypt into Canaan*. Cotton Mather called the Massachusetts Bay Colony "our American Jerusalem," and led the way in arguing that salvation of the Colony was the salvation of the individual American soul.

Bercovitch carefully traces the persistence of such politico-religious thinking down to the present day. Jonathan Edwards, John Adams, Harriet Beecher Stowe, and thousands of ministers from their pulpits, kept repeating the idea that God created America for the illumination of all mankind. Indeed many, such as Emerson, said so explicitly; and Henry David Thoreau added that if America were *not* the Great Western Pioneer whom other nations followed, then the world–let me say it again: the world–had no real purpose. The problem, of course, as one reviewer of Bercovitch's book put it, is that in practical terms, the myth boils down to not much more than the assertion "America right or wrong"–which made us, as Robert Kagan has written, a dangerous nation. In effect, Kagan argues that aggression is encoded in the national DNA;

that, to quote David Kennedy in his *Washington Post* review of Kagan's book, "the combination of material greed and moral righteousness is the soul of America's character and its foreign policy alike." The American report card, to use the language of elementary school, would be: Does not play well with others. To put it bluntly: If Kagan were describing a person, would you want them as your friend?

In any case, the myth of the City on a Hill, and all that this entails, is the foundation of the ritualistic and reflex thinking of Americans–the national orthodoxy, as it were. In 1967, when the myth was fueling our destructive involvement in Vietnam, Arthur Schlesinger referred to it directly, and not in a positive way. "The ultimate choice," he wrote, "is between messianism and maturity." But Americans can't seem to grasp this; maturity eludes them, endlessly. The very next year, when Robert Kennedy announced his candidacy for president, he declared that what was at stake was "our right to the moral leadership of this planet"–precisely the psychology that got us *into* Vietnam. There is simply no stopping this myth, and along with it, writes Baritz, comes a whisper, throughout our history, that other people really want to be like us, regardless of what they or their leaders say. As peculiar as it is, when you look at it from the outside, the basic American assumption is that the world is populated by potential Americans. Non-Americans often tend to regard this whole belief system as bizarre–as something akin to medieval possession, which is in fact a fairly good analogy.

Inevitably, the American belief in our quasi-religious mission brings with it an equally strong belief in our inherent goodness and innocence. Having no knowledge of the Middle East, or of the history of US foreign policy in that region, President Bush could wonder, in all honesty, how 9/11 could have occurred, since "we are so good." "Why do they hate us?", bewildered Americans kept asking. Paul Wolfowitz fairly screamed on TV, "This is the United States, for God's sakes!", not realizing that from the viewpoint of the Other, that was precisely the problem. In his brilliant novel, *The Quiet American* (1955), Graham Greene effectively predicted the debacle of Vietnam as a result of American naïveté–a naïveté that leads to a massacre that the central figure, Alden Pyle, dismisses as being necessary for the ultimate goal of democracy. Pyle has no feeling for or even interest in the actual flesh-and-blood people of Vietnam. With the best of intentions, Greene effectively says, people like this are destroying other nations.

In the light of his book, it is interesting to read the responses of 110 army generals who served in Vietnam to a questionnaire sent out to them in 1974, many of whom referred to the problem of American ignorance. We lost, wrote one general, because of "our overinflated hypnosis with the myth of the American way." But the truth is that no one–or almost no one—can get elected president in this country unless he embodies that myth, and reflects that hypnosis. "Freedom is pitted against slavery," intoned Dwight Eisenhower in his first public address after his inaugural; "lightness against the dark." It is as though Americans have to have this Manichaean framework, this structure of negative identity, in order to function in the world.

The real problem with running a country on an unconscious religious basis is that introspection and self-correction, which is to say, emotional maturity and growth, become almost impossible. As Gore Vidal once remarked, "Americans never learn; it's part of our charm." And although he is hardly one to talk, Henry Kissinger's frank observation, that it is very difficult for an American to grasp a different point of view, is not without relevance here. For the belief in American exceptionalism, that we are a nation chosen by God, is inculcated into American children from age five, if not before. In school they say the Pledge of Allegiance, read textbooks from which any real questioning of the Republic is completely absent, and hear their teachers repeat some form of "we're number one" over and over again. Surveys of attitudes among American adults, in terms of the discrepancy between image and reality, show the results of this pretty clearly. For example, a study released by the World Health Organization in 2004 revealed that in terms of health care in the developed or developing countries, we're No. 37; but the average American believes our medical system is the best in the world (Saudi Arabia, by way of comparison, ranked 26th). Another poll discovered that whereas U.S. foreign aid amounts to 1% of the American budget, Americans typically believe it is 25%. The point is that we prefer myth to reality, and Americanism is our myth, our religion.

The filtering of all of this into our foreign policy has had disastrous consequences, because if you see yourself as good, by definition, and the Other as evil, by definition, you are then going to map that simplistic mythology onto the world, reality be damned. This is, of course, how we got into Iraq. The truth is that the world is quite a complex place, filled with lots of nuance. But a monolithic view of the world, fueled by a civil religion, is hard to resist, because of its psychological promise of filling the emptiness within. And it is all the more powerful for being, for most Americans, completely unconscious. Writing in the February 2007 issue of *Foreign Policy*, retired Army Colonel Patrick Lang states that "our foreign policy tends to be predicated on the notion that everyone wants to be an American," that "the entire world is embarked on the same voyage, and that we are the navigators showing the way to a bright future." This belief system, he concludes, "has become a secular religion, a religion so strong that any violation of its tenets brings instant and savage condemnation." In fact, the nation's secular religion surfaces in our conscious awareness only rarely and briefly, namely when the adventures based on it hit a brick wall.

3. The point at which American imperial ambitions really took off can be dated to the immediate postwar period. In his famous "long telegram" from Moscow to Washington, dated 22 February 1946, and in his subsequent essay in *Foreign Affairs*, George Kennan coined the word "containment" and argued—quite ironically, as it turned out—that the Soviet Union saw the world in black-and-white terms, could not be reasoned with, thought only ideologically, and thus had to be confronted "with unalterable counter-force at every point." The irony, as Kennan himself later recognized–he was nothing if not a very sophisticated thinker–is that this pretty much described the United States! In fact, he explicitly stated, years later, that we were using the Soviet Union to fill a void within ourselves. In his memoirs, Kennan claimed that what he had had in mind way back in 1946 was political rather than military containment, and that in retrospect he felt that he had launched a movement he later came to regret. He changed his mind regarding the so-called perimeter defense, ar-guing, by 1949, that not *every* part of the world was vital to American security, and that we couldn't oppose com-munism wherever it appeared or be intervening in other countries' internal affairs. The process of trying to main-tain an empire, he wrote, would generate the resistance sufficient to undermine it. Famous last words, as they say.

Kennan died in 2005, having been pushed aside by 1950 by far less subtle thinkers, and then spending the next 55 years, regrettably enough, as irrelevant–if not actually embarrassing–to the foreign policy establishment. One of these less subtle thinkers was Paul Nitze, Kennan's suc-cessor at the State Department, who authored the top se-cret document known as NSC-68. Unlike Kennan, Nitze was moving with the times. The Truman Doctrine conve-niently blamed the USSR for all the troubles of the world, and NSC-68 called for the perimeter defense, whereby every opposition to the United States was to be regarded as equally important. The Kremlin was seen as the great enemy behind the scenes; containment was defined in military terms; and "negotiation" in our minds effectively meant Soviet capitulation. Senator Arthur Vandenburg told President Truman that the only way of selling such a policy to the public at large was "to scare the hell out of the American people." Dean Acheson, Truman's secretary of state, said it would be necessary to start using dramatic language, such as "the free versus the enslaved world." As Douglas MacArthur later put it, the goal of the government was to keep the American people in a perpetual state of fear, in a "continuous stampede of patriotic fervor." The City on a Hill was about to get a large dose of adrenaline.

The result was an inability to understand nationalist movements, wars of liberation, or civil wars, because anything that deviated from our vision of the world was now defined as evil. Nationalism was often confused with communism, and we had suddenly made ourselves responsible for virtually every political event taking place on the planet, all of which were to be regarded as equally important in terms of our security. The Korean War was thus launched for symbolic and political reasons, for the country never constituted any kind of real threat to us. Indeed, General Bradley, then chairman of the Joint Chiefs of Staff, actually stated that America was becoming embroiled "in the wrong war, at the wrong place, at the wrong time, and with the wrong enemy." Kennan repeatedly sent warnings to the White House that we were misunderstanding the nature of Soviet communism, and that the decision to go to war was an error. But the Truman administration was impervious to reason, because myth had colonized its brain. Religious frameworks are inevitably binary: God and the Devil go hand in hand. If you are the City on a Hill, it becomes almost inevitable that you will view your enemy as a large, unified force.

Thus when Truman made the decision to put the Seventh Fleet between Formosa and China on 27 June 1950, he explained the action in terms of an abstract and undifferentiated "Communism." Yet there was very little unity between Russian and China, and Joseph de Rivera, in *The Psychological Dimensions of Foreign Policy*, remarks that "The Americans seem to have had more faith in the idea of international communism than the Chinese or Russian leaders ever had." Truman and his advisers insisted on believing that China took its marching orders from the USSR, and therefore that its repeated warnings could be ignored, since it was obvious that Russia didn't want war. So American troops crossed the 38th parallel, Kennan quit the State Department in disgust, and the Chinese went on to inflict a major defeat on US troops, in November of 1950. Yet even after the defeat, the Truman administration refused to consider any change in policy. Dean Acheson called the attack a Russian trap, and continued to speak of China, Russia, and North Korea as a homogeneous entity. As for Truman, he bitterly denounced the GOP and the "conservative press" as having played into the hands of the Soviets.

In a word, the City on a Hill was supposedly under siege; "send more troops" was the obvious answer. The result was the death of many thousands of American soldiers, a military and political stalemate, and a failure to learn anything real about the enemy. This scenario was repeated, *mutatis mutandis*, over and over again, notably in Vietnam, which resulted in the death of 2 to 3 million Vietnamese peasants, and later on in Iraq. To its everlasting shame, the United States got involved in the forcible overthrow of one democratically elected regime after another: Iran in 1953, Guatemala in 1954, and Chile in 1973, to name but a few. In his book *Overthrow, New York Times* reporter Stephen Kinzer documents the bloody record of the United States in this regard during the twentieth century, pointing out that these countries were simply defending their right to self-determination, but that we have never been able to see this as anything but anti-American, despite our own demand for self-determination in 1776. Out of a fanatical antirevolutionary ideology, one that insisted, in the face of all evidence to the contrary, that the Soviet Union was behind any and all opposition to America, and that everything was linked together in a worldwide conspiracy, we delivered millions of so-called communists—mostly peasants and civilians—into the hands of dictators and torturers.

Leaving aside the fact that there were real differences and conflicts between socialist countries, or countries engaged in struggles for independence, it is useful to ask to what extent the Soviet Union was a real threat. In fact, for internal political reasons of its own, the USSR needed us as a dark, monolithic enemy as much as we needed them. In that sense, we and the Russians co-created the Cold War. There were many within the State Department who knew all along that the Soviet economy was little more than a joke; some analysts contemptuously referred to the Soviet Union as "Upper Volta with missiles." Consider the fact that in the National Security Strategy of 2002, written by Condoleezza Rice, the Bush administration admitted that during the Cold war, we faced a "risk-averse adversary"– an admission that could never have been made during the Cold War itself. KGB archives that opened up as of 1991 reveal that the Kremlin's focus was on internal security, not on world domination, and that it regarded Germany, rather than America, as its greatest threat. Its modus operandi in the postwar period was for the most part cautious and reactive.

Why was America not able to see this? Why, for instance, did we pay so little attention to the fact that the Kremlin backed away from supporting Greek and Italian communists after World War II, for example? In 1989, the Joint Chiefs of Staff issued a lengthy report called the "Joint Military Net Assessment," in which it repeated the arguments made by George Kennan forty years earlier. "Since the 1940s," wrote the Joint Chiefs, "the Soviets have demonstrated hesitancy to use military power as a means to achieve their foreign policy goals...The primary Soviet concern...is the security and integrity of the Soviet homeland." The point is that many high-ranking individuals, including generals in the Pentagon, knew all this, but they couldn't make a difference because once again, myth does not yield easily to facts. The American psyche badly needs its founding myth, and an oppositional structure, so as to have a sense of meaning in the world.

4. It was for this reason that the fall of the USSR left us completely disoriented. When Mikhail Gorbachev declared that the Cold War was over, we had no place to stand. We had been playing the game of City on a Hill vs. evil empire for so long, that the collapse of our negative identity revealed the lack of a clear-cut positive one. George Bush, Sr. was completely at a loss, and tried to fill the void by finding another war. First was the so-called War on Drugs, which cost us $20 billion and led to nothing; and then came a temporary stopgap, the Gulf War of 1991. Saddam Hussein was stupid enough to do the wrong thing at the wrong time and in effect get caught in American existential anxieties.

The first Gulf War was really an accidental war; we cared as much about the people of Kuwait as we did about those of, say, Micronesia, and we were certainly not dependent on Kuwaiti oil. But if on the mythological level you need to be pursuing a messianic goal, then your psyche is constantly scanning for targets, and up popped Iraq on the radar screen. We had never cared about the internecine feuds within the Arab world unless they were of strategic advantage to us, and in fact, as is now well known, the Bush, Sr. administration gave Saddam Hussein a green light to invade Kuwait. Shortly before the invasion, the American ambassador to Iraq, April Glaspie, following the administration line, told Hussein that Arab border disputes were not things we intended to concern ourselves with. Of course, when Iraq actually did attack Kuwait, it was an opportunity for us, on an unconscious level, to fill the void with this new "enemy." However, as with the putative "War on Drugs," the Gulf War had no staying power; it didn't fit into any clear post-Cold War pattern. Bush, Sr. kept going on about the "new world order," but these were just buzzwords to him; he didn't really understand the significance of the events happening around him, and his confusion was quite palpable. He himself stated that he had no vision, and he was easily pushed aside.

Bill Clinton's solution to the sudden loss of negative identity was the historical alternative to what might be called the crusader state: let's all make money. Now *there's* a vision for you! I don't have time to get into this alternative strand in our history, which is certainly not a minor theme: the Puritans wrote at the top of their business ledgers, "For God and Profit." I suppose the clearest articulation of this theme is Calvin Coolidge's famous declaration, "The business of America is business." "It's the economy, stupid!" was Clinton's campaign slogan, and when he got into office his focus was on the passage of NAFTA, "growing the economy," the "information highway," and "globalization," which the out-of-office neoconservatives contemptuously referred to as "globaloney." To borrow a phrase from Jerry Seinfeld, the Clinton presidency was a show about nothing. Consumerism worked for a time, but ultimately it lacked the grand mythological appeal of the city on a hill or a crusade against an evil empire. When they weren't glued to their TV screens watching the trial of O.J. Simpson, or that of Clinton himself, most Americans, it would seem, were just flailing around, trying to fill the void with shopping or by investing in the market—a bubble that burst with the dot.com collapse at the end of the nineties. Meanwhile, the neocons hung out in the wings, bided their time, and waited for the opportunity to get some version of the Cold War back. In fact, the first document along these lines, claiming a need for the United States to take over Iraq, secure the Middle East, and essentially dominate the world, was drafted in 1990 and 1992 by Paul Wolfowitz, then Under Secretary of State. It got leaked to the *New York Times* in March 1992 and was dismissed by politicians on both sides of the aisle as basically the ravings of a lunatic. But it hardly went away, finally showing up in September 2000 as a ninety-page pamphlet called "Rebuilding America's Defenses," and sponsored by PNAC, the Project for the New American Century, which was the neocon crowd. What was "lunacy" in 1992 became mainstream government policy a short ten years later. What had intervened, of course, was 9/11. The PNAC report states quite candidly that Saddam Hussein was nothing more than an "immediate justification," or pretext, for a larger goal, namely that of controlling the Gulf region. But, it adds, there is no way to put this into practice "absent some catastrophic and catalyzing event—like a new Pearl Harbor." (More famous last words.)

It was this particular sentence in the report that fueled the conspiracy theory about 9/11, that it was really an inside job—I get asked that question virtually every time I give a public lecture. I don't believe it myself, nor do I believe that the war protesters, with their signs that said "No Blood for Oil," got it right either. After all, we were getting a mere 11% of our oil imports from Iraq prior to 2003, much less than we were getting from, say, Venezuela. But all of that is not my point here. My point is that given the whole configuration of American mythology and negative identity, and the meaninglessness in which America floated between 1991 and 2001, 9/11, horrible as it was, was from another angle literally manna from heaven, giving the nation Meaning again with a capital M. Overnight, Bush, Jr. was using words like "evildoers" and "crusade"; his rhetoric was completely apocalyptic. In fact, the National Security Strategy of September 2002, to which I've already referred, declares that we shall "rid the world of evil." What was perhaps inspiring and touchingly naive in Puritan New England now had the flavor of naked megalomania, or even mental illness. As the British journalist George Monbiot predicted even before the release of the NSS, "If the United States were not preparing to attack Iraq, it would be preparing to attack another nation. The United States will go to war because it needs a country with which to go to war."

Commenting on our current inability to extricate ourselves from Iraq, William Pfaff, in an article published a few years ago in the *New York Review of Books* (15 February 2007), remarks that the real stumbling block is that "It is something like a national heresy"–note the choice of words here–"to suggest or admit that the United States does not have a unique moral role to play in the world." The corollary, of course, is that no political figure can endorse anything that smacks of a defeat. Pfaff concludes by saying that none of our current foreign policy debates raise a challenge to the notion of the United States as having a special national mission; and that while a different

(Democratic) administration would probably be more suave and courteous in its conduct of U.S. foreign policy, we can expect that the overall ideology will remain intact—something that has proven to be 100% true. There is, he says, too much investment in the national myth for us to be able to reverse course.

5. What did we do after 9/11? We took the easy path. We chose to believe that the attacks emerged out of a political vacuum, not, to use the jargon of the CIA, that they were "blowback" for U.S. foreign policy in the Middle East. In fact, Osama bin Laden had been articulating Muslim grievances against the United States for years: massive support for Israel, and practically nothing for the Palestinians; stationing U.S. troops on Saudi Arabian soil, not far from Islamic holy places, for twelve years; support for political regimes that oppress Arab peoples—the list is rather long, and was characterized as quite justified by no less a figure than Michael Scheuer, who was the CIA's Osama expert for seventeen years. Over and over again, bin Laden in effect said, You screw with us, and we'll screw with you—which is of course what finally happened.

But rather than trying to understand Arab rage against America, we seized upon the old Manichaean formula of the Cold War, simply replacing the word "communism" with the word "terrorism," so that we could continue to fill up the empty space within. Same story, different cast of characters. We created a shinier, more improved monolith, with a new set of buzzwords such as "globalist jihad" and "Islamofascism," which obscure any possible nuance or complexity. In other words, we have once again manufactured a monolithic template to map onto the world, and the result of this is plain for all to see. Bush didn't even know that there was a theological and political conflict between Shiite and Sunni Muslims until the night before the 2003 invasion of Iraq, when he was briefed by an Arabist expert from the State Department. The result is a civil war between the two factions, a Vietnam-style quagmire, and very likely, a Vietnam-style American loss. The myth of the City on a Hill, and the apparent need we have to force democracy down people's throats whether they want it or not, is undermining what is left of the City on a Hill.

Personally, I don't believe the timing of the attack on the World Trade Center was accidental; after all, one dials 911 in the United States in cases of emergency–the symbolism is rather obvious. By failing to grasp the meaning of 9/11, we managed to convince ourselves that what was in fact profound structural weakness was instead the apex of American power. This is a tragic confusion, and it will cost us dearly. "Rome,"writes Harvard University's Joseph Nye, "succumbed not to the rise of a new empire, but to internal decay and the death of a thousand cuts from various barbarian groups." If the meaning of 9/11 was a wake-up call, the lesson of 9/11 is that we learned nothing at all.

As for the logic of opposition, and its role in filling the void, this was never better captured than by the Greek poet, Constantine Cavafy, in his 1904 poem, "Waiting for the Barbarians." Cavafy describes the Romans, assembled in the Forum, waiting for the barbarians to show up at the gates. They wait and wait, but the barbarians fail to come. Cavafy concludes:

> Why this sudden bewilderment, this confusion?
> (How serious people's faces have become.)
> Why are the streets and squares emptying so rapidly,
> everyone going home lost in thought?
> Because night has fallen and the barbarians haven't
> come.
> And some of our men just in from the border say
> there are no barbarians any longer.

> Now what's going to happen to us without barbarians?
> They were, those people, a kind of solution.

References

Robert Bellah, "Civil Religion in America," *Daedalus*, No. 96 (1967), pp. 1-21.

Morris Berman, *Dark Ages America* (New York: W.W. Norton, 2006).

H.W. Brands, *The Devil We Knew* (New York: Oxford University Press, 1993).

Ivan Eland, *The Empire Has No Clothes* (Oakland: The Independent Institute, 2004).

Robert Kagan, *Dangerous Nation* (New York: Vintage, 2007).

Frank Rich, *The Greatest Story Ever Sold* (New York: Penguin, 2006).

Jeffrey Sachs, *The End of Poverty* (New York: Penguin, 2005).

6. The Real Gold

I confess I never gave much thought to Colombia during most of my life; or at least, not more than I did, let's say, to Kenya or Bangladesh. Real ignorance on my part, to be sure (familiarity with the work of Gabriel García Márquez notwithstanding); but my impressions of Colombia were formed by the American (U.S.) media, so what typically came to mind when the country was mentioned were drugs and violence. Then suddenly, a few years ago, I received an invitation to speak in Bogotá, so I just decided to suspend any prejudgments I had and get on the plane.

The occasion was a *lanzamiento*, or "launching" of the second edition of a book of mine that had been translated into Spanish a few years back. During the week of my visit, my sponsor, whom I'll refer to as Juan, arranged a dinner at which I would be able to meet a number of distinguished writers from the Latin American world. These were folks who had won an international competition–drawing on Colombia, Spain, Mexico, and Venezuela–and who had, as a result, come to Colombia to give a week of workshops to aspiring writers. We met, all ten of us, at a fairly elegant restaurant in downtown Bogotá, at about 8:30 p.m.

It was a delightful evening. What was most striking to me was the ambience, the energy that moved around the table. Put a collection of leading writers, academics, businessmen, artists–practically anybody, really–together in the United States, and what you frequently wind up with is a bunch of aggressive egos competing to be Number

One. The conversation will be subtly boastful, filled with witty put-downs and a kind of controlled (or not-so-controlled) narcissism that is so common in the United States that we don't even notice it; anthropologically speaking, it's just part of the air we breathe. These Latinos, by contrast, were gracious, *suave*, and low-key. They joked a lot, reflected on art and literature, and obviously enjoyed each other's company. I couldn't help thinking that whereas so much ritual interaction in the United States seems to have a tacit agenda or subtext of promoting oneself at the expense of others, the interaction among this group was about respecting each other, making everybody feel valued. It's a cliché, of course, but sometimes you can't see the "given" of your own culture until you are confronted with the "otherness" of another one.

Dinner over, we all shook hands and parted. Juan and I and another writer, Alberto, walked out of the building and onto the street. As Alberto walked away, I noticed he was rather overweight and walked with a slight limp. There was something very human about this; something real and vulnerable. And then, he unexpectedly turned toward me and said, quite simply, "Bienvenidos." It was casual, but nevertheless very poignant: deliberate inclusion of the outsider; recognition.

A couple of days later, having some free time on my hands, I decided to visit Bogotá's famous gold museum, the Museo de Oro. Actually, I was finding it a bit boring. Anthropological significance aside, gold just doesn't turn my crank, even when it is artistically crafted. Standing in front of one display, I looked around to discover that I was surrounded by something like fifty schoolchildren, ages twelve to sixteen, all in uniform. Three schoolgirls moved closer to me; the most "courageous" asked me if I had the time. I showed her my watch. *"Tres y diez,"* I tell her. "Are you a visitor?" she continued (she's now eight inches away from me). I was suddenly aware that what was happening would strike an odd note in a U.S. context. For one thing, Americans are not terribly interested in foreigners, as far as I can make out; until recently, when it became officially required to have a passport to re-enter the United States from Canada or Mexico, only 12% of U.S. adults owned one. And American schoolgirls would not be likely to approach a white-haired man in his sixties unless it was part of an inside joke. I was startled by the simplicity and directness of this encounter; clearly, this young lady had every right to be taken seriously. We chatted for a while, as two of her girlfriends listened in, intently. I told her I was a writer from the United States, here to talk about one of my books. I asked her what school they were all from (San Agustín), and what the class subject was (anthropology). Finally, we stopped talking and just smiled; I touched her lightly on the shoulder and said, "Adios."

About an hour later I was sitting at the entrance to the museum, indoors, at the far end of a low stone ledge, writing these notes, when my three new "friends," along with the rest of the horde, swept through the lobby. They all crowded onto the ledge, the three girls making a point of plunking themselves down right next to me, causing me to scramble to shove my briefcase and jacket out of the way, so as to make room for them. Two of the girls were hugging each other, which I found rather touching, and–again–something one just doesn't see in the United States. The "courageous" one looked over at my notes.

"¿Qué escribe?" she said, looking up at me. I couldn't very well tell her I was writing about her and her friends, so instead I asked her what other class trips they had all been on. "This one is the first," she said, "but next month we're going to the planetarium." I asked her what she thought about gold; she just shrugged. "Perhaps the stars will be more exciting," I suggested. She laughed. At this point their teacher announced that they needed to leave, and they all stood up to go. As they swarmed away, the two younger girls, who were still hugging each other, turned around and looked back. "Bye," one of them said in English, smiling at me. "Bye," I replied. The hall emptied out; it was suddenly silent again. I sat there, thinking about the sheer innocence, the natural friendliness, of the whole interaction–interaction of a kind that no longer seems to be part of the U.S. social landscape. How much, I thought, we have lost, without even realizing it.

So I didn't find any drugs or violence in Colombia, though I am well aware that they are there. But I couldn't help reflecting on the possibility that there are different types of violence in this world, and that the relentless destruction of "social capital," as Harvard sociologist Robert Putnam calls positive human interactions and relations, has to be one of the most pernicious forms, especially when it seems to permeate an entire society (sort of like odorless gas, or like something that got put into the water supply). What have we Northerners paid in return for our extreme individualism, our constant competition, and our sad confusion of "goods" with "the good life"? Sociologist Robert Bellah puts it this way: "Our material success," he writes, "is our punishment, in terms of what that success has done to the natural environment, our social fabric, and our personal lives."

I guess there's no turning back now.

7. Ik Is Us: The Every-Man-for-Himself Society

Although I was born in America, I am only first generation, my family having emigrated from eastern Europe in 1920. As a child, I was raised in what might be called a European socialist ethic: you help other people. As a result, I lived, in the United States, in a state of perpetual culture shock for nearly six decades. It didn't take me very long to figure out that it was by competition, rather than by cooperation, that American society worked. Not helping other people is systemic in the United States; it is literally woven into the fabric of American life, if not actually into our DNA. It's not a question of immorality as much as amorality: we aren't raised with an ideology, or even a consciousness, in which the other person counts. I remember, when I was fifteen years old, some boy in my school whom I knew only vaguely–his name was Tom—was walking around on crutches after knee surgery. Much to my surprise, he asked me if I would carry his books for him from his home room to his first class, as he couldn't manage to do this while on crutches. I did it for two weeks, until he was able to do it himself, and didn't think twice about it. About a week into this routine, Tom's mother called mine. "You know," she said, "Tom asked about a dozen students, including close friends of his, and they all said that they couldn't do it because they didn't want to be late for their first class. In my opinion, your son is a saint." "My son is not a saint," my mother fairly snorted, stating the obvious; "he's just doing what he's supposed to be doing."

Fast-forward forty-five years, and now *I* have had knee surgery and am returning home from the hospital on crutches. As I approach the side door of my building, someone who also lives in the building is coming down the walk, busily talking on his cell phone. He looks at me briefly, then takes out his plastic pass key, swipes it in the little magnetic coding box, opens the door and goes in. The door shuts behind him; I'm standing outside of it, now fumbling in my wallet to find my own plastic entry card. Suddenly, the man–apparently seized by a rare moment of human fellow-feeling–pushes the door open from the inside. He doesn't come out and hold it open for me, mind you; he just pushes it open, so I can sort of squeeze myself into the doorway on my crutches. He then hurries down the hall to the elevator, leaving me in the dust, as it were. Not a word is exchanged.

A few months later–the end of August 2005, to be more precise–I have an appointment at the University of Maryland Hospital in Baltimore, and need to check out the men's room before I take the elevator upstairs. I walk in on a scene in which a man has collapsed on the floor, and someone else is trying to get him up on his feet. "Hold on," I say; "I'll go get help." The first person I see outside the men's room, about six feet away, is a police officer sitting on a bench. "Can you help?" I ask him; "some guy just collapsed on the floor of the bathroom." "I don't work here," he replies; "go to the In-patient Desk." Given the emergency nature of the situation, I don't bother to argue with him about the irrelevance of his nonemployment for helping someone in distress, but take off for the In-patient

Desk. "Can you help?" I ask the woman at the desk; "a man has collapsed on the floor of the bathroom down the hall." "You'll have to talk to Security, over there," she gestures. I run over to the Security officer, repeat the story for the third time. "I'll call the Fire Department," he says. What relevance the Fire Department has to somebody passing out in the bathroom I have no idea, but I just say, "It's this way." He is already walking ahead of me, and when he reaches the men's room, he keeps on going. "Here!" I shout; "it's right here." He just keeps walking down the hall. I figure the guy is probably dead by now anyway.

A few days later, hurricane Katrina struck New Orleans. As we all know, the response of the Federal Government was very slow: for several days, people were left to fend for themselves, and vast numbers were without food or water. During this time, a friend of mine, a lawyer, sent me an online video that was made by MSNBC the day after Katrina hit the city, showing people looting a Wal-Mart store. This in itself was not that shocking; basically, it's what I and probably a lot of other Americans would expect. What *was* impressive was the fact that the police were also there, wheeling shopping carts around and looting right along with the looters. When Martin Savidge of NBC News asked one policewoman what she was doing, she replied, "Jus' doin' mah job." Apparently, stealing DVD players while the townspeople were drowning was not a problem for New Orleans' Finest.

Is the reader beginning to notice a pattern here? In one form or another, this is America in microcosm, and it is disturbingly reminiscent of the worldview of the Ik of Uganda as described by the anthropologist Colin Turnbull in *The Mountain People*. This tribe had been reduced to a condition of savage self-interest due to economic hardship. Turnbull describes how, when a member of the tribe died, neighbors (as well as children and siblings) would fight over the person's few belongings, and then abandon the corpse. Turnbull comments that in this system of mutual exploitation, affection and trust were actually dysfunctional. "Does that sound so very different from our own society?" he asks at the end of the book. These words were written in 1972; one can only wonder what Turnbull would have thought of American life thirty-odd years later, were he still alive. What, after all, can be the fate or future of a country in which people on crutches constitute an annoying distraction; in which the hospital staff response to a man collapsing on the floor is, "It's not my problem"; and in which the police join looters in their looting while all around them people are dying by the thousands?

Any ideas?

8. The Black Hole of Bethesda

Occasionally I get a letter from a reader of my *Twilight of American Culture*, complaining that history and sociology are all well and good, but that I should give the public more of the actual details of the decline of the United States.* They are right, of course, the more so since we swim in the raw data of the latter on a daily basis. A recent encounter with the American medical establishment provided me with clear evidence that "twilight" is hardly an abstract concept.

My regular doctor, a very intelligent, white-haired gentleman of the old school, also happens to be a gastroenterologist, and so is always on my case about having a colonoscopy. ("I'm lucky you're not a neurosurgeon," I once kidded him. "Would be too late in your case anyway," he shot back.) He had given me one six years ago, when I briefly had a real job and therefore had real health insurance; but one reason I kept putting it off was that as a free-lancer, I was now paying a high monthly premium for insurance that was, in the crunch, worthless. Somehow, my insurance company always had a reason why this particular claim (whatever it was) was not covered, and I could either let it go—my usual choice, since arguing with them was pointless—or appeal it, in which case I would get a check for $50 or so six months later. So I kept telling him I couldn't afford it, until he finally offered to cut me a deal. "I usually get a grand for the job," he said; "I'll do it for you for $600. In addition, you should call the surgery facility in Bethesda and tell them that for a significant reduction in price, you'll pay them up front. Finally, you can try to negotiate with the anesthesiologist, who also charges a grand."

So I took his instructions. I called Judy at the surgery facility; she told me that if I brought the cash in an envelope, she'd drop the cost from $1000 to $470. As for anesthesia, I decided to go without, and save myself at least $600, probably more. "I don't recommend it," my doctor said; "the procedure takes about fifteen minutes, and without anesthesia it's going to hurt." "Hey," I told him, "a total of $1070 out of pocket is already more than I can afford; I'm a writer, you know what we make." "Your call," he shrugged.

Two months later, the day before the procedure, I called Judy once again. She had no memory of our conversation, so I had to tell her that we had agreed upon $470, and that there would be no anesthesia. "I'm sorry I can't remember; I just dropped my daughter off at the testing place, where she's taking her SATs. I'm concerned about her doing well, so I guess I'm not thinking very clearly." "No worries," I told her; "they now add something like 200 points for free. All American high school kids are now above average, so I'm sure she'll do well." She laughed. "Yeah...I know, you're right." "Listen," I said, "why don't you take down all my data now, so that when I come in tomorrow, I won't have to do reams of paperwork." She agreed, noted the various meds I was on and so forth. "See you tomorrow," she said brightly.

I arrived the next day, and handed Judy $470 in a plain brown envelope. It felt like hush money, or some sort of payola. Then they took me back to the pre-op room; it turned out that there was no record whatsoever of yesterday's phone conversation with Judy, so I had to repeat everything I had told her the day before, including the bit about no anesthesia. Then my doctor came in. "How's it going?" he asked. "Fine. Listen," I said, "you're doing me a favor by cutting me a deal, so I'm going to write you a check right now, before we get started." He grunted; I handed him a check for $600. He pointed to the OR. "See you in there when you're ready."

So next I'm lying on the hospital cot, hooked up to a monitor, and he's telling me about his vacation in Germany and Switzerland as he's poking my anus. "OK, here we go." Before too long I was screaming. It seems that there's no problem when the plastic tube traverses straight colon, but when it goes around a bend—watch out. While I was screaming, I couldn't help wondering if the U.S. government had ever thought of employing this technique at Guantánamo or the American "gulag" of torture sites, as Al Gore once referred to it. It was unbearable, and of the fifteen minutes I spent on the cot, I probably screamed for three. In the middle of this, my doctor's cell phone went off, and he took the call. I tried to say, "If it's for me, tell them I'll get back to them later," but I was too busy screaming. "Can't talk right now," my doctor said, and rang off. I guess I should have been thankful for that.

Finally, it was over. I got off the cot and slowly made my way back to the pre-op room to dress. My doctor stuck his head in. "Doing OK?" "Yeah...I guess so. Say, it says on this sheet the nurse gave me that I need to make a follow-up appointment for two weeks from now." He waved his hand dismissively. "Don't bother with that, since we're economizing here"; meaning: we only schedule those things to make more money, but since you are relatively broke, I'm not going to screw you. "See you in five years," I said.

Out in the waiting room, the receptionist handed me an envelope. "Here are your personal effects," she said. I looked at it closely: "Seymour Hockenhauser" was clearly printed at the top. "I'm not Seymour Hockenhauser," I told her, handing it back. "Oh," she said, "didn't you give me anything?" "I guess not," I replied. "Have a nice day," she said.

I dragged my sorry ass out to the parking lot. One advantage of not having anesthesia is that you get to drive yourself home.

*At this point the sequel to *Twilight, Dark Ages America* (New York: W.W. Norton, 2006), had not yet appeared.

9. Massacre at CNN

On 16 April 2007, on the campus of the Virginia Polytechnic Institute in Blacksburg, Virginia, a 23-year-old student, a Korean national by the name of Cho Seung-Hui, shot and killed thirty-two students and professors, and then shot himself. For the next two weeks, all the major television networks covered the story in detail, and then, as with everything else in the news, it dropped out of sight, in this case being replaced by discussions of profit earnings at Microsoft.

I was traveling through Mexico (Tabasco and Chiapas) at the time, so my only access to information, besides the local newspapers, was CNN. In a weird way, the CNN coverage was as peculiar as the event itself. The focus was entirely on who this person, Cho Seung-Hui, was; the larger context in which the event took place—and there have been quite a few in recent American history—was never even referred to. Of course, if you focus on how aberrant Cho was, then the larger context becomes (supposedly) irrelevant and can be ignored; which is certainly what the media, and the American public, want. So we learned that Cho was Korean, not American; a loner, depressed from an early age; a psychotic, obsessed with death and weaponry (as one sensationalist video, which CNN kept playing over and over, revealed), and so on. CNN also conducted a fatuous interview with Cho's former roommates, trying to probe into his relations with women and his sexual proclivities. Other coverage included the usual handwringing after such incidents, suggestions from some journalists and "experts" that students and professors need to come to classes armed; the appointing of a commission to investigate the event, etc.–the usual suspects, in short, which has never amounted to anything in the past and didn't this time either.

CNN did, however, briefly refer to some sort of suicide note left by Cho, in which he apparently talked about the pretensions of the wealthy students at the school, and the "charlatanry" that pervaded the campus. The news network also read an email from someone in Korea, who pointed out that Cho was, green card notwithstanding, an American: he had come to the United States with his parents when he was eight years old, and had thus spent two-thirds of his life in an American context, being exposed to American values. "An incident such as this [massacre]," the writer concluded, "has not occurred in Korea during its 5000-year-long history." This too was passed over by CNN, a topic they obviously preferred not to deal with.

Of course, I never personally saw Cho's suicide note, so I can only guess at what went on in his mind, or what led him to kill thirty-two innocent people. But the brief reference to the contents of the note, the letter from the Korean writer, and the endless focus on Cho himself as alienated and insane, suggest a few things that were not part of the CNN coverage. To take an extreme analogy, there would seem to be an odd similarity between this coverage and that of the 9/11 attack on the World Trade Center. Network news "analysis," if such it can be called, was all about Osama bin Laden and Mohammed Atta as "evil" and "insane." When Susan Sontag subsequently made a brief comment in the pages of the *New Yorker* to the effect that U.S. foreign policy might tell us more about the causes of 9/11 than the psyche of Osama bin Laden, a national uproar ensued, in which she was basically branded a traitor. Any serious student of U.S. postwar activity in the Middle East knows that Sontag's comment was totally on target; but the desire of the media, and the American public, to preserve an image of American innocence vs. external evil is too powerful to allow even a hint of an alternative possibility. In the case of the Virginia Tech massacre, I am not (as in the case of 9/11) suggesting that the slaughter of civilians is justified; of course it isn't. But as in the case of Susan Sontag's commentary, I do think that what happened at Virginia Tech might be *explicable*, and that a deeper understanding of the event beyond "the killer was insane" might be worth having. Consider, then, the following:

1. Cho Seung-Hui, at age eight, left a society that has not had such a civilian incident in its 5000-year history and entered a society in which violence, via movies, television, and basic daily life, is the norm. This was his true socialization as a child, adolescent, and young adult. Just to take one statistical example, a U.S.-Canada survey taken in the year 2000 revealed that while 12% of Canadians said Yes to the question, "Is it acceptable to use violence to get what you want?", 24% of Americans answered in the affirmative. Or if we consider the world data on homicide, the average rate of homicides per 100,000 people in the European Union was 1.7 during 1997-99, while the U.S. rate

during the same period was 6.26, or nearly four times that number. The homicide rate for American children during that period was five times higher than for the children of the next twenty-five wealthiest nations in the world combined.

2. What Cho also saw around himself, in addition to violence, was "charlatanry," as he apparently put it. This strikes me as about as great a revelation as the fact that the Pope is Catholic. American society is totally opportunistic, epitomized by TV shows such as "Survivor." As Karl Marx put it long ago, the bonds of friendship and community get dissolved in "the icy waters of egotistical calculation." It's all Los Angeles, in the United States: everybody has an agenda, an ulterior motive, which is the core of their individual "program" of self-promotion, and which they regard as the purpose of life. Someone coming from a society that still, in some ways, has traditional values, can't help but be disgusted at what passes for human relations in America. As the historian and social critic Paul Fussell once wrote, "everything in the United States is coated with a fine layer of fraud."

3. Of course, there are literally millions of immigrants who come to the United States, absorb the violent messages that exist all around them, see the charlatanry that pervades the American Way of Life, and don't go on a killing rampage. In that sense, individual psychology might indeed be more helpful than mass sociology, but only if your goal is to answer the question, Why this particular individual? But there is, surely, a deeper question, namely:

Why aren't a lot more individuals doing something similar? The large per capita intake of Prozac and other tranquilizers might offer one possible answer, of course, in that these drugs enable the American population to suppress its rage. But the society that generates the rage remains the crucial, and unacknowledged, point. And this is the truth that CNN seeks (consciously or unconsciously) to keep out of the public eye. As a result, the "understanding" it provides is self-serving and skin-deep. How many other societies, Japan excepted (which is a whole other discussion), are plagued by chronic outbursts of seemingly apolitical violence against innocent bystanders? The fact is that these outbursts *are* political, if "political" is expanded to include the nature of the culture at large, and the way in which it works at its most basic level.

One final example of what I am talking about. During the vapid CNN interview with Cho's former roommates about his sex life, a caption ran at the bottom of the TV screen, telling the viewers that this interview was available only on CNN. And there we have it, in a nutshell: the goal of every American institution is (or supposedly should be) to be Numero Uno. In the midst of a massacre, of the brutal deaths of thirty-two innocents (including Professor Livriu Librescu, a Holocaust survivor who apparently had to come to an American college campus to finally get himself liquidated), what's important to CNN is that they be first with the scoop. Death makes absolutely no difference to these people; that the charlatanry continue, is what counts for them. Everything is marketing in the United States, everything is promotion, and I submit that this is what probably pushed Cho over the edge. That CNN couldn't even see the irony of what they were doing, finally says it all.

10. The Structuralists

> Limbo is our Way of Life.
> –William Appleman Williams

The word "structuralism" is commonly associated with a group of French intellectuals who were prominent in the sixties and seventies, and whose work, which was based on linguistics, came to dominate the human sciences for a good many years. Indeed, Michel Foucault, Jacques Lacan, Claude Lévi-Strauss, and Louis Althusser constituted a veritable galaxy of talent. Although one can find numerous academic texts explaining what structuralism is, the philosophy (or mode of analysis) can be summarized as follows:

1. Every system, whether it be a novel or a civilization, has a structure, i.e. is characterized by deep underlying patterns.
2. That structure is more significant than the individual elements of the system, and in fact determines the position or role of the elements in the system.
3. In any system, continuity is much more common than change, and that continuity follows the "map" provided by the deep underlying patterns.
4. Structures are the "real things" that lie beneath the surface phenomena, or appearances (cf. the distinction between light and shadows in Plato's Parable of the Cave).

Understood in this way, it seems fair to assert that structuralism is not the exclusive property of the French.

For example, although structural analysis is not typical of U.S. intellectual circles, a few American scholars have nevertheless used it in their research to great effect. I am thinking of four writers in particular, whose work, when integrated into a comprehensive whole, provides a radically different picture of the United States than the one commonly held: the land of freedom and opportunity. It is not likely that many Americans would be able to tolerate this alternative structuralist view of American history, although they needn't worry, inasmuch as anything even mildly resembling it remains very far removed from public discussion. Thus for most Americans, Vietnam was an unfortunate "mistake"; Iraq is part of the effort to "spread democracy" (but now in the process of being reclassified as a mistake); September 11th was the result of enemies who are "evil" or "insane"; and the economic crash of October 2008 was the product of individual greed, the work of a few (perhaps even quite a few) "bad apples". None of these sorts of events (which could, in fact, be multiplied indefinitely) are seen as being endemic to the system, to the American Way of Life; as following inevitably from its underlying structure. That would, needless to say, be a wake-up call of the first magnitude.

The four scholars I have in mind probably never met, and for the most part (not entirely) were ignorant of each others' work. These are the historians William Appleman Williams (d. 1990) and Joyce Appleby, to whom we have already referred; the philosopher Albert Borgmann; and the Chilean-born writer and journalist Ariel Dorfman (who has lived and worked in the United States for several decades now). Ostensibly, they don't have all that much in common, having directed their attention to very diverse topics. But as indicated above, when you put them together you get a picture of the United States that forms a coherent whole, one that most Americans would find very disturbing to contemplate. As the saying goes, they don't teach this sort of thing in school.

To begin with Williams, then: 2009 marked the fiftieth anniversary of his most famous work, *The Tragedy of American Diplomacy*. In this book, Williams argues that the expansionist or imperial tendencies of the United States were present from its earliest days. American political leaders, he writes, believed that the doors to economic expansion had to be open in order to secure U.S. democratic institutions. They couldn't imagine the American people living within the limits of their own resources. And the American people, he goes on to say, were thoroughly on board with this program. Whether we are talking about farmers or workers or the middle class, they all shared an ideology of informal imperialism. Empire, in a word, was seen as essential to the good life. In particular, the Founding Fathers regarded territorial expansion as key to keeping American society from congealing into a European class system. But there was a price to be paid for all of this, and it was not a small one. For what the frontier did, according to Williams, was take us away from what was essential—a fair and just society, organized along the lines of democratic socialism. Instead, there was a collective (if unconscious, I would add) decision to run away from this, and thus to run away from (real) life. In *The Contours of American History* (1961), Williams puts it this way:

> Americans...have the chance to create the first truly democratic socialism in the world. That opportunity is the only real frontier available to Americans in the second half of the twentieth century. If they...acted upon the...intelligence and morality and courage that it would take to explore and develop that frontier, then they would finally have broken the chains of their own past. Otherwise, they would ultimately fall victims to a nostalgia for their childhood.

I shall return to this theme of childhood in a moment. For now, let us be clear about the conundrum that Williams identified: the choice between individual capital accumulation, or obsession with private property, and a more equitable capital distribution, or concern for the collective well-being of the nation. Williams traced this fundamental conflict back to England's Glorious Revolution (1688), by which time it was clearly understood that expansion was the only way to reconcile these opposing ways of life. In the American context, it took the form of an addiction to the frontier as utopia. As a result, there really *was* no positive vision of commonwealth. In the nineteenth century, says Williams, the focus was on expansion, pure and simple, at the cost of social and personal values. To put it bluntly, Americans have always relied on expansion to escape from domestic problems, and resorted to violence and aggression when this failed. Williams was fond of quoting James Madison on the subject: "Extend the sphere and you have made it less probable that a majority of the whole will have a common motive to invade the rights of other citizens."

According to Williams, then, the United States was caught in a kind of balancing act, in which outward movement—territorial conquest, market expansion, or war—became the default solution to all of its domestic ills. Empire would reconcile avarice and morality. You defuse demands for a redistribution of wealth by opening up "surplus social space." "We have been playing hide-and-seek for two centuries," he wrote in 1976; "limbo is our Way of Life."

Still, it is not clear what Americans are running from; it is probably deeper than democratic socialism, and at one point Williams argues that we are afraid of our own violence. Whatever this dark presence is, it has to run very deep, because as Williams shows, anything that stood in the way of expansion—Native Americans, the Confederacy, the Soviet Union, and finally the Third World—was regarded as "evil," unnatural, beyond redemption. Looking inward, looking at ourselves, was never a serious option, and examining the structures that underlay its behavior was never America's forte.

Before we can ascertain what Americans are running from, however, it will be necessary to get some idea of how they wound up in a state of internal conflict and competition in the first place. On the surface, it seems almost as though aggression, narcissism, and imperialism are literally woven into the country's DNA; as though, in the United States, life and greed are synonymous. As we have seen, the shift from a European-based sense of commonwealth to a me-first free-for-all dates primarily from the 1790s.* Until that time, according to Joyce Appleby, the idea of a greater good and a system of reciprocal obligations still carried some weight, and the word "virtue" was defined as a commitment to those things. Under the impact of the ideas of Adam Smith and the Scottish enlightenment, however, this began to change. The new, Newtonian-based philosophy held that societies were collections of individuals ("atoms"), and that the pursuit of profit on the part of each of these entities combined–i.e. the collective result of individual self-interest–would be the prosperity of the whole. "Virtue," in other words, had by 1800 come to mean personal success in an opportunistic environment; looking out for Number One.

The result was that the glue that had held colonial life together began to disintegrate, for individual greed is basically an antiglue. Historically speaking, according to Gordon Wood, this constituted a complete transformation in human social relations, amounting to a very new type of society. One might even call it an antisociety. Contemplating these developments in the early years of the Republic, the Philadelphia physician Benjamin Rush was forced to conclude that the nation "would eventually fall apart in an orgy of selfishness." The reality of contemporary America would undoubtedly shock Dr. Rush, were he to return from the grave, but it probably would not surprise him.

(As an aside I offer the following anecdote: a friend of mine who happens to be the dean of a major medical school in the United States read Appleby's work some time ago and was very impressed with it. But he discovered that whenever he tried to discuss her thesis with members of the faculty, their eyes would glaze over within thirty seconds and they would change the subject. I believe this attests to the massive brainwashing prevalent in the United States, such that even the nation's most intelligent citizens literally cannot tolerate even a casual examination of the country's structural premises.)

In any case, the U.S. Census Bureau declared the frontier closed in 1890; there was no more unclaimed land to be had. Having stolen half of Mexico in 1848, the United States really couldn't now lay claim to the rest of that country, so it began looking farther afield for new conquests. Thus, the Spanish-American War of 1898, and the formulation of the Open Door Policy in 1899, which asserted the importance of overseas economic expansion. Yet the real frontier of the so-called Progressive Era was internal, which is to say, technological—a conception that has lasted down to the present day. For this development we need to move on to the third figure on our list, Albert Borgmann, whose *Technology and the Character of Contemporary Life* takes the work of William Appleman Williams to the next level.

In some ways, Borgmann was anticipated by the historian David Potter, who recognized (in *People of Plenty*, 1954) that Frederick Jackson Turner's famous "frontier thesis," while correct, didn't have to be conceived of in strictly geographical terms. The *psychic* frontier in the United States, he said, is based on the interaction between technology and the environment, and hence the promised expansion is without limit. This had actually been made explicit by the first presidential scientific adviser, Vannevar Bush, in his definitive essay of 1945: *Science the Endless Frontier*. But the basic structural mechanism–expansion as a way of mitigating domestic conflict–was in place long before Potter or Bush arrived on the scene. "Commodity expansion," to coin a phrase, was merely the old structure of Manifest Destiny mapped onto a different field; and as Borgmann demonstrates, it "works" even better. For there isn't, and there will not be, an end to the gizmos and gadgets the consumer society can crank out. Where there are now ten varieties of razor blades, there will be twenty tomorrow, and fifty a year from now—all "new and improved," with advertising serving to convince us that all of this junk is essential to our lives. From Milton Friedman to Condoleezza Rice, drowning in crap is regarded as "freedom," with virtually no dissent on the subject from the American people.

Here is a definition of democracy provided by a former American ambassador to Brazil (1961-62), Lincoln Gordon, in his book *A New Deal for Latin America*:

> True democracy...is the regime of continuous social revolution. I use the word revolution to mean a process of structural change in society—an alteration in the pattern of social class, in the social mobility of individuals and their children, in the educational structure, in methods of production,

standards of living, and the distribution of income, and in attitudes toward relationships among individuals, business and other private organizations, and the State.

Sounds pretty good, right? A far cry from the stagnant, class-based society of medieval Europe, to be sure. But what it amounts to in practice–if we leave aside the reference to distribution of income, which strikes an odd note here–is the society Joyce Appleby described and Benjamin Rush decried: an endless jockeying for position and power. And what fuels this social mobility, as Borgmann recognized, is constant invention and innovation, so that the lower class believes it can acquire the goods and lifestyle of the middle class, and the middle class believes it can acquire the same of the upper class. In *Dark Ages America* I wrote:

> The privileges of the ruling class are exercised in consonance with popular goals. Rich and poor both want the same things, and in this way commodities...are the stabilizing factors of technological societies. Social inequality favors the advancement of the reign of technology, in other words, because it presents a ladder of what can be attained through technology. This results in an equilibrium that can be maintained only by the production of more and more commodities. The less affluent must be able, at least in theory, to catch up with the more affluent. Hence politics remains without substance, a realm from which the crucial dimensions of life, the core values, are excluded.

In reality, this "escalator" of social mobility is an illusion. Very little wealth "trickles down," and the statistics are quite clear on this point: the vast majority of the population never escape from the class into which they were born. But the combination of techno-economic expansion, and stories of the "self-made man," are sufficient to keep the lid on the conflict and hostility that are generated by endless competition. Meanwhile, our lives are filled with toys as substitutes for friendship, community, craftsmanship, quality, an equitable distribution of wealth, and an enlightened citizenry as opposed to a large collection of child-consumers who have literally no idea as to what genuine political debate is about. "Growth" is all... but to what end? This is the question that almost never gets asked.

The matter of children and their toys brings us to the fourth author, Ariel Dorfman, who formulated the concept of "soft power" long before Joseph Nye of Harvard University coined the phrase. What Dorfman asked was this: What makes American culture so popular, worldwide? Why is everyone attracted to its omnipresent symbols—Mickey Mouse, Coca-Cola, McDonald's, blue jeans, American sitcoms, and the like? What a paradox, that so many nations despise the United States while the citizens of those nations are literally addicted to American television programs. What, in short, is America's secret?

Dorfman is a Marxist, yet he surprised himself when he realized the decidedly non-Marxist answer to this question: "The way in which American mass culture reaches out to people may touch upon mechanisms embedded in our innermost being." In a word, the appeal is archetypal, transhistorical, and transcultural. For human beings are biologically programmed to respond to anything tinged with childhood. We seek to protect our young; we have tender feelings toward them. Mickey Mouse effectively joins power and infantilization, as does virtually all of American culture. That culture broadcasts a message of rejuvenation, a fountain of eternal youth, and (says Dorfman) "the possibility of conserving some form of innocence as one grows up." Whereas previously the U.S. Army was the means of exerting influence, the mass media now becomes a "peaceful" way of extending the American frontier. In fact, it is far superior to "hard power," because it enables Americans to retain an image of themselves as innocent, and to not have to recognize that this is just another version of imperial expansion. "America was able to project a universal category–childhood–onto alien cultures that were subjected politically and economically, and to seek in them infantile echoes, the yearning for redemption, innocence, and eternal life that, to one degree or another, are part of the constitution of all human beings." But when the American is shorn of adult faculties, adds Dorfman, and "handed solutions that suckle and comfort him...what is left is a babe, a dwindled, decreased human being."

The recent remarks of third-party candidate Ralph Nader, who could never manage to garner more than a tiny fraction of the vote, are quite relevant in this regard: the new generation of Americans, he said, "have little toys and gizmos that they hold in their hands. They have no idea of any public protest or activity. It is a tapestry of passivity."

But the problem goes way beyond toys as a political substitute. It is all part of remaining a child, and of renewing
or "reinventing" oneself through the latest electronic gadget or new consumer product that rolls off the assembly
line. (One could include New Age gurus and philosophies
in this list as well.) And even beyond this, the notion is
that all of the world can be renewed by turning it into one
huge market place, or toy store. What else, after all, is life
about–for a child?

This, then, is the heart of "soft power," that empire
and childhood are linked by an endless succession of new
toys; a world in which every day is Christmas, and in which
the neurosis of the United States becomes the power of
the United States, as every last human being on the planet
is sucked into this vortex. The American empire, in reality, is an Empire of Children.

We are now, I believe, in a position to answer the
question of what all of this frenetic activity is designed to
hide; what Americans are running away from. Toward the
end of his life Williams wrote: "America is the kind of culture that wakes you in the night, the kind of nightmare
that may [yet] possibly lead us closer to the truth." This
is a haunting, if enigmatic, sentence. What truth, after
all? Possibly, an example of what *not* to do. For the truth
here is an emptiness at the center, to which is added a desire to never grow up. It should be obvious by now that
the American definition of "progress" is little more than
a joke, and that running away from the responsibilities
of adulthood–including the construction of a society not

based on endless consumption, competition, and expansion—could be the single greatest thread in American history. That there is a possible alternative history, and a very different type of progress, characterized (for example) by marginal figures such as Lewis Mumford or the late Jane Jacobs, is something Americans don't wish to contemplate, for alternatives to the life of running faster to get nowhere scare them. No, the expansion game, and the life of limbo, as Williams puts it, will continue until we hit a wall, and the game cannot be played any longer (although I suspect we shall be able to limp along with "crisis management" for two or three more decades). This game, of self-destruction and the destruction of others, will continue until there is no place for America to go except to the graveyard of failed empires. And as Williams suggested, violence is very likely part of the equation.

In the meantime, much of the world, ironically enough, will go on taking the United States as a model for development, ignoring the bankruptcy of this way of life. The sadness of it all was captured by Richard Easterlin in his incisive study, *Growth Triumphant*: "In the end, the triumph of economic growth is not a triumph of humanity over material wants; rather, it is the triumph of material wants over humanity." Once expansion fails, however, the jig will be up. Whether Americans will finally address the thing they've been hiding from all these years is another question altogether.

The widespread emulation of this model is thus a peculiarly depressing aspect of the whole drama. I wrote this article in Mexico City, and being late for a meeting with a friend, shut my notebook and grabbed a taxi to get to my rendezvous on time. The driver, a young man of about twenty-five years of age, stared into the screen of his cell phone or blackberry while weaving through traffic. As I glanced over his shoulder, I saw that he was looking at cartoons, of the kind I watched on television when I was seven years old. Finally, nervous that he was going to plow into the truck in front of us, I asked him whether watching a screen while driving wasn't just a little bit dangerous. "Oh no," he told me, never taking his eyes off the screen; "not a problem." Meanwhile, he overshot my destination, had to consult the map I had with me, and wound up charging me twice as much as the ride would normally cost. I wasn't in the mood to get into a long argument with him in Spanish about it, so I paid the fare and wished him buen día. But I couldn't help thinking what a jackass this kid was, and, at the same time, that what was in his head regarding the components of a meaningful life was probably not very different from what was in the head of the president of any Mexican or American or (for that matter) Indian university or corporation. Clearly, the psychology of expand-and-hide spreads like cancer: "growth" *über Alles*.

We see, then, the picture of the United States that emerges when we look at it structurally. Put Williams, Appleby, Borgmann, and Dorfman together, and it is as though you are looking at America with X-ray eyes. "Freedom" and "Opportunity" are not what stand out, on this view. Rather, the X-ray vision reveals something much closer to disease, what has been called an "ideological pathology." Living in limbo, as Williams told us over and over again, cannot be prolonged indefinitely. Yet the real tragedy, in my view, is not one of American diplomacy but of willful ignorance. Is it likely, when the system finally unravels and the empire is a feeble shadow of its former self, that we (or the hegemon that replaces us) will have learned anything at all?

*This is not quite true. Walter McDougall, in *Freedom Just Around the Corner* (New York: HarperCollins, 2004), says we were a nation of hustlers (his word) from the get-go; and Richard Bushman documents this for eighteenth-century Connecticut in *From Puritan to Yankee* (New York: W.W. Norton, 1970). See below, Essay #20.

References

Keith Berwick, review of Williams, *The Contours of American History*, in *The William and Mary Quarterly*, January 1963, pp. 144-46.

Paul Buhle and Edward Rice-Maximin, "War Without End," *The Village Voice*, 5 November 1991, p. 75.

Ariel Dorfman, *The Empire's Old Clothes*, trans. Clark Hansen (New York: Pantheon, 1983).

Greg Grandin, "Off Dead Center," *The Nation*, 1 July 2009.

Chris Hedges, "Nader Was Right," posted on www.truthdig.com, 10 August 2009.

William Fletcher Thompson, Jr., review of Williams, *The Contours of American History*, in *The Wisconsin Magazine of History*, Winter 1962-63, pp. 139-40.

Frederick Jackson Turner, "The Significance of the Frontier in American History," lecture to the American Historical Association, Chicago, 1893; reprinted in numerous anthologies and available at www.historians.org/pubs/archives/Turnerthesis.htm.

Gordon Wood, *The Radicalism of the American Revolution* (New York: Vintage, 1993).

11. A Show About Nothing

One of the most successful sitcoms in the history of American television was the show *Seinfeld*, which debuted in 1989 and ran continuously through 1998. The principal scriptwriters, Jerry Seinfeld and Larry David, originally pitched it to NBC as "a show about nothing," because their idea was that the individual episodes would have no plot and instead focus on the trivia of everyday life. For the most part, they stuck to the plan, and the show proved to be hysterically funny. It was also, I'm proud to say, very much a case of *Jewish* humor, which some might argue is humor at its best. As Freud pointed out in his famous book *Jokes and Their Relation to the Unconscious*, a joke is never just a joke; it masks a subtext, an intention that is typically very different from what is being overtly expressed. And in the case of Jewish humor, that subtext is almost always sad, depressing, or even tragic. The function of the joke is to ease the pain.

My maternal grandfather, who virtually raised me, told lots of jokes of this sort. He even compiled a book of aphorisms, based on the east European oral tradition, ones that had this kind of twist to them. (It was published in Wilno, Poland, in Yiddish in 1930.) One of his favorite jokes—it may have even been a true story, for all I know—was about a man who went to his doctor for his annual checkup. The doctor examined him, took blood, etc., but was unable to collect a urine specimen because the man did not have the urge to go at that particular moment. "Drop it off tomorrow," the doctor told him. The man went home, got up the next morning, peed in a jar, and then had a bright idea: the family was too poor for everyone to have a medical exam; why not have them all pee in the same jar, so that unbeknownst to the doctor, the entire family could get analyzed at the same time? So the wife and children were added to the mix, and as the man was leaving his house to go to the doctor's he decided he might as well throw in a sample from the family horse, which was tethered to a tree in the front yard. He then brought the jar to the doctor's office. "Come back next week," the doctor said, "and I'll give you the results." The man left and returned in seven days. "Everything seems to be fine," said the doctor; "the only thing I would recommend is that you cut down on your intake of oats."

Funny, yes? But the humor masks a situation that was daily fare for the Jews of eastern Europe: extreme poverty. In fact, my grandfather told me that at one point the family managed to survive by eating the plaster off the door jambs of the house they were living in. Nothing funny about that.

In the case of the *Seinfeld* scripts, Jerry provided the upbeat, overt aspect of the show's humor, while Larry David supplied the subtext. Larry's vision, especially about America, was quite dark. As a result, there is an undercurrent in the episodes, one which says that the United States is a country in which friendship is pretty much a sham and community nonexistent; a society where nobody gives a damn about anybody else. This is true not only in the way that the four central characters–Jerry, Elaine, George, and

Kramer—relate to those outside their little circle, but also in the way they relate to each other. They often talk simultaneously, "through" each other, as though the other person weren't even present. All four of them appear to have only one motive: advancement of their own personal and immediate goals. In a word, the show is actually about the callousness, the almost autistic indifference, of daily life in America; and this is revealed in episode after episode. Just off the top of my head, the following vignettes come to mind:

-Elaine and Jerry are sitting in a coffee shop when they are approached by a man who explains that his son is a big fan of Jerry's, and loves watching him when he appears on TV. It turns out that the boy has some rare immune-deficiency disorder that requires him to live in a hermetically sealed plastic bubble. As he talks about his little "bubble boy," the man begins to weep. Elaine, also crying, reaches for the napkin holder and hands napkins to the man and Jerry. She and the man wipe their eyes; Jerry, who is calmly munching on a sandwich, matter-of-factly wipes his mouth.

-George and his girlfriend Susan drive north from New York City for a holiday weekend at her grandfather's cabin. George gives Susan money to pay the tolls en route. It turns out that Kramer visited the cabin a bit earlier and accidentally left a lit cigar behind—one that Susan's father had given to George, who in turn had given to Kramer. By the time George and Susan arrive at the cabin, the place is engulfed in flames. Susan screams, "Oh my God, the cabin!" George turns to her and says, "I just remembered: I don't think you gave me the change from the money I gave you for the tolls."

-A scene at a funeral, being held for an acquaintance of Jerry's and Elaine's who was killed in an auto accident. They are sitting in church (or synagogue), waiting for the service to begin. In the background, we hear the periodic sobbing of the family members. Elaine turns to Jerry and says, "I really have to get some new clothes. I'm bored with everything I have." Pause; more sobbing, which is now much louder. "Really," she continues, "I have absolutely nothing to wear."

-Another funeral, this time for one of Jerry's relatives. Elaine is hell-bent on getting the deceased's rent-controlled apartment. As she moves forward in the receiving line to express her condolences, she finally shakes the hand of an elderly relative of the deceased, who happens to be hard of hearing, and yells in his ear, "So what about the apartment?"

-George is attending the birthday party of his current girlfriend's little boy. At some point, someone burns a hamburger in the kitchen, and smoke starts pouring out the kitchen door. "Fire!" yells George, "Fire!", as he makes for the front door of the house, knocking over elderly women and little children in his path.

-As if to deliberately mock the notion of community (or lack thereof), there is an episode in which Kramer takes photos of everyone in the building and posts them, along with the corresponding name of each person, on the wall of the foyer, just inside the entrance. The idea is that the residents will now be able to greet each other by name. The whole thing is too phony to be believed, especially when the tenants begin kissing one another when they meet–a common practice in Mexico and many other countries, but totally inappropriate in the United States. Jerry, who can't stand the bullshit involved, opts out, refusing to kiss and hug, and thereby becomes the target of public hostility.

All of this reaches a kind of climax in the very last episode of the show, in which Larry David in particular makes his opinion of the nature of American life quite clear. In this ninety-minute finale, the Gang of Four are arrested in Massachusetts for ignoring a (nonexistent, in real life) "Good Samaritan Law," whereby one is supposedly required to come to the aid of other people in distress. They are put on trial, and practically everyone from the show's nine years of episodes flies into this small New England town to watch the proceedings or actually take the witness stand and describe to the judge and jury how abusively they had been treated by the gang. It is at this point that the *Seinfeld* episodes are revealed for what they were all along: all of these vignettes had something very ugly underneath them. Other people were merely pawns in (or obstacles to) Jerry's, Elaine's, George's, or Kramer's personal agenda. Humor aside, the vision of here American life is quite bleak. When Jerry phones his lawyer, "Jackie Chiles" (a Johnnie Cochran look-alike), to explain that they were arrested for not coming to someone's aid, Jackie explodes with indignation: "Why, that's ridiculous!" he barks. "You don't have to help *anybody*. That's what this country is all about!" As the popular American expression has it, He got that one right.

The trial over, the judge sentences our heroes to a year in jail, commenting that "your callous disregard for other human beings threatens to rock the very foundations of society." But which society? What the show tells us, in episode after episode, is that callous disregard for other human beings *is* the foundation of society—American society, that is. And so the subtext finally breaks through in no uncertain terms: *Seinfeld* was A Show About Something, after all.

12. Spheres of Influence

Some time ago, the opportunity to do a silent five-day retreat at a Benedictine monastery presented itself. In the past, I had done long meditation retreats of a Buddhist nature, but I had never done anything in a Christian context before, so I decided I should give it a try.

The monastery, which I shall call Our Lady of Silence, was located in the back woods of Mexico, in the middle of nowhere. The grounds were incredibly beautiful, dotted with agave and cactus, nopal and mesquite. Burros and sheep wandered across the landscape, which was so quiet you could almost hear the butterflies winging past you. Except for the occasional hum of crickets, the stillness was literally absolute.

This beauty extended to the architecture as well. The new church, cloister, and refectory were built only a few years ago, with a kind of simple, modern design that nevertheless captured the harmony of the Middle Ages, complete with wooden beams and stained glass. Seven monks and a priest constituted the permanent residents; most of them were in their late twenties. At one point, I remember looking across the table at one older monk, with his cropped hair, carefully trimmed beard, and pensive aura, and thinking that I must have seen him before, in some medieval woodcut.

Hours are observed here with great regularity: Matins at 4:30 a.m., Lauds at 6:30, mass at 7, breakfast at 8,

Terce at 8:50, lunch at 1:25 p.m., Nones at 2:30, Vespers at 5:30, dinner at 6:45, Compline at 8:10. I went to Vespers every day; the chanting of the monks was so gentle, it was as though they were singing love songs, like the troubadours of the twelfth and thirteenth centuries.

And it was, in fact, like living during that time; really, like living in a kind of glass sphere. No outside news entered the monastery. There was no TV or radio, no newspapers or journals of any kind. I wondered if the monks knew who the current president of Mexico was, let alone of the United States.

I had brought a couple of books of a spiritual nature along with me to read, but other than that, I had decided to follow the monastic example and stay cut off from the outside world: no news magazines, history books, transistor radios, or anything of the kind. As a result, the silence, and the empty space, got filled up with the contents of my psyche. Material spontaneously started drifting upward, as it were. Within two hours of arriving at the monastery I had a major breakthrough, unraveling something that I had been emotionally wrestling with for several weeks.

Two other experiences stand out. One was coming into the refectory at dinner and sitting down in front of what looked like a blue corn patty, mixed in with nopal. As I picked up my knife and fork, one of the monks slipped a CD of *Ave Maria* into the stereo system. The sounds filled the hall; I wavered, suddenly on the verge of tears, not able to eat for two or three minutes. (I later learned that the monks were worried I might be staging a protest against the food. The patty did, in fact, require a large dollop of *salsa roja* in order to liven it up.)

The second was "accidentally" locking myself out of my cell at 6:20 in the morning, on the way to the bathroom. My first reaction was: *Oh dammit to hell.* But then I was grateful that I was dressed and wearing clogs, and carrying a flashlight; it could have been much worse. Unfortunately, I had forgotten to put on my glasses, and I am terribly nearsighted. I also realized that this annoying event was probably not an accident: I had been embroiled in identity issues for three days now, and keys are a symbol of that. Whenever these types of issues arise for me, I typically lose my keys or wallet, or lock myself out of my car, and/or have a dream about these things. I should have known, I thought. In any case, what was there to do, in the near-freezing cold, except climb the hill up to the church and sit through Lauds and the mass? At least, I consoled myself, it was warm in the church.

I had been to mass only once before in my life, Christmas Eve 1973, at the Église St.-Séverin in Paris, a thirteenth-century structure that sits adjacent to the Sorbonne. It had been exquisite; it's a wonder I didn't convert to Catholicism right then and there. The mass at the monastery was also "Parisian," but in a rather different way: without my glasses, I couldn't see much beyond blobs of color—an Impressionist mass, as it were. When it was over, I approached one of the monks with my problem, and he immediately got the master key and let me back into my cell.

The day before, I had been rereading one of the books I brought with me, *What We May Be*, by Piero Ferrucci. Ferrucci is an Italian psychotherapist, a student of Roberto Assagioli, who founded a school and technique known as Psychosynthesis. It has much in common with Jungian analysis, in fact. The section I had been reading deals with beauty.

> Music has a powerful effect on several bodily rhythms and functions and on psychological states...neural networks in the brain may be responsive to harmonic principles in general. And there is such a factor within us as an "inbuilt urge to maintain a state of intellectual and aesthetic order and harmonic balance, essential to mental health."*
>
> But we do not need research to know that the magnificence of a cathedral's rose window, the design of Celtic manuscripts, a flower in full bloom, or the perfect geometry of a Greek temple does not leave us unaffected. And the moment we let ourselves be touched by beauty, that part of us which has been badly bruised or even shattered by the events of life may begin to be revitalized. At that moment a true victory takes place–a victory over discouragement, a positive affirmation against resigning ourselves to the process of crystallization and death. That victory is also a step forward in our growth in a very precise and literal sense, for the moment we fully appreciate beauty we become more than we were. *We live in a moment of pure psy-*

chological health. We effortlessly build a stronghold against the negative pressures that life inevitably brings.

But that is not all, for all stimuli–beautiful or ugly–sink into the unconscious, where their influence becomes less immediate, but more powerful and pervasive....

When stimuli of the same kind are repeated a number of times–as in the case of the 15,000 killings the average American adolescent has seen on TV**–their effects multiply and come to generate a real psychological climate in the inner world of the individual....

We can be[come] exposed to what Assagioli called "psychic smog"–the prevailing mass of free-floating psychological poisons....

Earlier I referred to the monastery as a kind of glass sphere, hermetically sealed. If it keeps out the news of the modern world, it also keeps out the garbage of that world as well. It is a sphere of harmony, of beauty, designed to bring peace to the soul. As for the modern world, in particular the America of endless violence and "psychic smog," Ferrucci follows up the above quotation with a reference to a famous painting by Hieronymus Bosch, in which the sixteenth-century artist "depicts the damned of Hell as being enveloped by an opaque crystal ball, impeding all communication with the outside world."

And this is, very unfortunately, a fair description of the United States. As several of the essays in this collection clearly demonstrate, Americans live in a kind of hologram, or glass sphere with mirroring on the inside. Literally every thought they have is on the order of a programmed response, dating from the early years of the Republic: "chosen people," "City on a Hill," "civil religion," "endless frontier," "rugged individualism," and so on. For more than two centuries now, the same slogans and buzzwords have bounced around inside the sphere, mirroring and confirming each other. Contradictory information–represented, for example, by the *analysis* of that sphere and its mental processes–is never allowed to get through. The result is the smog or poison Assagioli talks about: a culture that is not merely stupid (and stupefied), but remarkably violent, all the while celebrating how "superior" it is to all the rest–and certainly, to some medieval throwback in the hinterland of Mexico, right? In fact, when you think about it, American society is no less hermetically sealed than the world of a medieval monastery; only the content is different.

I couldn't help thinking of a film I had seen shortly before coming to the monastery, *Crossing Over*, about the U.S. Immigration and Customs Enforcement (ICE) and its persecution of alien residents, legal as well as illegal. But it proves to be about much more than the daily activities of the ICE. By the end of the film, you realize that you have been watching an X-ray of the American soul, and you are struck dumb by how violent it is, down to its very core. Destructive as well as self-destructive, it reflects a culture in a state of fear, on its last legs, lashing out at helpless victims and imaginary enemies alike. The "toxic cloud" Don DeLillo described many years ago in his brilliant novel,

White Noise, now seems to have arrived in full force. This is psychological poison at its worst (or close to it).

I left Our Lady of Silence determined to carry the silence with me into my daily life: gardening, walking, meditating more, whatever. But the key issue, of course, is not my own personal life, but the dichotomy, the problem of the two separate spheres. Very few of us are cut out to live in a monastery, after all. All beauty aside, it's not a solution for the modern world. Yet what kind of solution—to anything—is U.S. corporate-commercial culture? That much of the world seeks to emulate it doesn't change the fact that it amounts to little more than trash, "psychic smog" that is slowly (and sometimes rapidly) killing off its inhabitants (who nevertheless can't seem to get enough of it). If there is a third sphere, a serious institutional alternative to these two that exists in practice, not just theory, I have yet to see it. And without that, what kind of future do we finally have?

*Quotation is from a 1977 article by Anthony Trowbridge.

**Written ca. 1980; we can expect that the current number is by now four or five times that amount, especially if we add in input from movies, DVD's, computer games, and the Internet.

13. Democracy in America

Since American democracy is in the process of dis-integration, it might be worthwhile to reflect on the nature of the phenomenon, and the sources of its dialectical death. In 1982 the eminent French scholar, Pierre Manent, published a study of Alexis de Tocqueville's *Democracy in America*, the two volumes of which came out in 1835/40. Manent's work was subsequently translated into English under the title *Tocqueville and the Nature of Democracy*; Harvey Mansfield of Harvard University contributed a Foreword to it. Mansfield writes:

> Democracy produces a sense of independence in its citizens, a sentiment that each is a whole because he depends on no one else; and the democratic dogma [nota bene] states that every citizen is competent to govern his own life. Hence democracy is not merely, perhaps not primarily, a form of government; or it is [a] form of government that almost denies the need for government. And as a society, democracy is antisocial; it severs individuals from one another by pronouncing each of them equally free. All the traditional relationships are broken or weakened.... Above all, democracy does not know where it tends and where it should go.

The blurb on the back cover of the book states that "Pierre Manent's analysis concludes that the growth of state power and the homogenization of society are two primary consequences of equalizing conditions." We are, of course, living with these consequences 175 years later.

Prof. Mansfield is, as one would expect, a proponent of democracy; most Americans are. Yet one wonders what he thinks of his own critique; the characteristics he identifies don't exactly amount to minor drawbacks in the system. I couldn't help looking at it through the lens of Islamic societies (to the extent that I am able to do such a thing). Quite obviously, I'm not a big fan of Allah's, nor of stoning of adulterers to death, nor of intellectual stultification, etc. etc., and I suspect it will be a fairly long time before I put down a deposit on a condo in Tehran. But their problems don't do anything to improve our own, and it seems to me that their revulsion toward the United States is not all that puzzling, if one considers the following points:

-"each is a whole because he depends on no one else"
-"a form of government that almost denies the need for government"
-"democracy is antisocial; it severs individuals from one another"
-"all the traditional relationships are broken or weakened"
-"democracy does not know...where it should go"

Clearly, with friends like these (Mansfield), democracy needs no enemies; this is a fairly good description of a "psychological slum," as Philip Slater once called the United States. And speaking of enemies, I couldn't help thinking of the message to the American people delivered by Osama bin Laden on the eve of the 2004 presidential election. I don't have the text in front of me at the moment, but I remember his saying, "You have no Guide, no Helper." He understood that America was a ship without a rudder—something that the two candidates, G.W. Bush and John Kerry, were unable to grasp. They both condemned the address without any substantive comment, to show they were "tough on terrorism"; thereby losing the opportunity to reflect, publicly, on what bin Laden was saying and what had gone wrong with American democracy (which of course wouldn't have gone over well with a basically stupefied electorate—and indeed, one of Tocqueville's major points was that democracy ultimately wouldn't work if the population wasn't too bright.)

Mansfield's critique also meshes well with the recent book by Jacqueline Olds and Richard Schwartz, *The Lonely American*, which documents the lives of quiet desperation that Americans lead. Nationwide, 25% of all habitations are single-person dwellings, and the figure for New York City is nearly 50%. In recent years the number of people who say they don't have a single person they can confide in has jumped to 33%, if I remember correctly. It's a sad, if honest, book—an obituary, really, for a bold and brilliant experiment that finally didn't work out. For suicide takes place on two levels: the macrolevel, of public institutions and domestic and foreign policy; and the microlevel, i.e. in the hearts and minds of individual citizens.

Finally: I have always been a great admirer of Isaiah Berlin, the Russian-Jewish-British political scientist who spent his life cautioning the West about the dangers of coercive systems such as that of the former Soviet Union.

In his famous Oxford University inaugural lecture of 1958, "Two Concepts of Liberty," Berlin defined "negative freedom" as freedom *from*; it is the freedom to do whatever the heck you please as long as you don't infringe on anyone else. "Positive freedom," on the other hand, is freedom *to*; it is the freedom of a directive ideal, one that holds up a vision of the good life (whatever that might be) and encourages—or forces—people to conform to that image. Going back to at least the seventeenth century, negative freedom is the Anglo-Saxon conception of what it means to be free; and as far as Berlin was concerned (as a good British subject—he became Sir Isaiah the year before his inaugural lecture), that was the only real freedom around; the other variety, he argued, was inevitably dangerous. The only problem is, without a positive vision of the good life, the good society, what are we? How could we be anything else except a ship without a rudder? This, to me, is the Achilles heel in the Berlinian edifice, for negative freedom finally affirms nothing—as the example of contemporary America clearly demonstrates. George H.W. Bush, that great intellectual, was fond of using the word "vision" sarcastically; he was proud of the fact that he had none. (What a shock, that his son became an alcoholic and a Christian fundamentalist.) He was a synecdoche for the nation, and ironically, he confirmed what Osama bin Laden said about the United States a dozen or so years later.

There is no doubt, of course, that "vision" can get out of hand; this was Berlin's whole point. But what he failed to understand was that lack of vision can also get out of hand, as Harvey Mansfield makes abundantly clear. And that has happened in the United States, which accounts for the odd combination in our contemporary political life of hysteria plus inertia. It also means that there is no way of reversing the trajectory; I mean, where do you start? You can't just assign the country "vision," and think that's going to work (this was in fact the idea of the communitarian movement of the nineties, led by Amitai Etzioni, and it was an embarrassing failure). The dialectical part of this is that the strengths of American democracy are precisely its weaknesses; the whole thing is a package deal. Or to put it another way, the ideology of negative freedom, of no-vision, cannot evolve into anything else but the negative, visionless society that we now have, and the seeds of this were planted a long time ago.

So here we are, wrote T.S. Eliot in the *Four Quartets*, "in the middle way...years largely wasted, the years of *l'entre deux guerres*" (obviously more than deux, in the case of the United States),

> And so each venture
> Is...a raid on the inarticulate
> With shabby equipment always deteriorating....

The *Four Quartets* is about many things, but I believe Eliot's major theme here is the acceptance of death. Wouldn't it make sense, at this point, for America to "resign" with dignity? To come to terms with the dynamics of its collapse, and just accept it? To finally (to quote another famous poet) "go gentle into that good night"? I expect that kind of maturity is completely beyond our grasp, but it would be, at long last, a vision of sorts.

PART II
MIND AND
BODY

14. Love and Death

> In everyone there sleeps
> A sense of life lived according to love.
> –Philip Larkin, "Faith Healing"

A few years ago an American journalist wrote that "The death instinct hovers over the United States." I had known this for some time, of course; when you turn yourself into a late-empire killing machine, what other outcome could there be? But the phrase "death instinct," so stark and Freudian in its implications, really caught my attention. Long before Freud, poets and novelists had written of the intimate connection between love and death, *Eros* and *Thanatos.* Indeed, when the former gets blocked or thwarted, it turns into the latter, its opposite. Check out the body language of Dick Cheney or Condoleezza Rice, if you don't believe me.

Since the 1960s, America has been seen as the land of hedonism, the place where "anything goes." But the truth is that this is a thin veneer placed over a much deeper Puritan reality. "Scratch an American," wrote one astute historian in the late sixties, "and you find a Puritan." It's much worse now than it was forty years ago, of course; "political correctness" is nothing if not a Puritan movement. Thus I was recently contacted by a German journalist living in Washington, D.C., who expressed her horror at a number of current news items. One involved a situation in which the parents of a two-year-old had their child playing in their backyard, in a diaper, and the next-door neighbors called the police to report this case of "indecent exposure." The police, instead of suggesting that the neighbors check themselves into the nearest mental hospital, came to the parents' house and ordered them to put some clothing on the child.

Another situation she reported to me involved that of a six-year-old boy who wrote a note to a classmate, telling her "I love you." The little girl showed the note to her parents, who then descended on the school principal, choking with anxiety. The principal could have pointed out how sweet this love note was, how touching. Instead, he inflicted permanent emotional damage on the little boy by suspending him from school for three days. Clearly, hatred of life is a terrifying thing.

The flip side of this, as battalions of sociologists have pointed out, is pornography. By this I don't mean merely the tons of pictures and videos on the Internet, but, along with the militarization of American life, the sexualization of it. Sex permeates the public sphere in the United States in a way that is impossible to avoid. Television, advertising, films, you name it—sex is somehow always present. And yet, what does it really come down to? Recent studies of American sexual behavior reveal that actual sexual activity is way down, from years past; Americans are too busy working and consuming to have time for pleasure in their lives. Pornography is something that takes place in the mind, and since almost all of it is variations on a theme, it's actually quite boring. All it amounts to is a kind of mental "utopia" that never manages to get below the neck. Many years ago Octavio Paz wrote that North Americans were big on pornography because they didn't really live in their bodies; that in the United States, the life of the senses had atrophied.

I remember when I first visited Mexico, in 1979. The most striking thing about crossing the border was the explosion of color. Prior to that, the color range I was used to consisted of varying shades of gray and green. Suddenly, I felt like the victim of a visual assault: Mexico was a riot of color. Houses of deep blue, ochre, salmon, brilliant yellow—what a feast, I remember thinking. True, I had had somewhat similar experiences in San Francisco, New Mexico, and Italy, for example, but this was much more dramatic; it seemed to be a statement about reality, about the nature of things. As I traveled around Mexico, I remember thinking: Which country really has the wealth? What *is* "wealth," when you get right down to it? Thirty years later, I live in a Mexican house whose walls are so drenched in color that I see no point in putting up any pictures. The walls themselves are the "art."

And of course, if there is very little repression of sensuality in Mexico, there is also very little repression of death. Since North Americans don't really live, in a sensual or erotic way, death is a great source of fear for them, a taboo subject. (The guy who wants the party to go on forever is the one who never had the courage to approach the pretty girls.) In Mexico, on the other hand, death is never very far from one's consciousness. Pictures of skulls, skeletons, national holidays—all of this seems ever-present, reminding us that you'd better enjoy life while you can, because it's over pretty quickly, and you are going to be dead for a very long time.

"Make love, not war," the Austrian psychiatrist, Wilhelm Reich, told us many years ago, in so many words. I guess the old boy knew what he was talking about.

15. The Lure of Other Worlds

The essence of man is desire.
    –Spinoza

At one time or another, all of us ponder the notion of happiness–what it consists of, and how to achieve it. This is my own small contribution to this great question.

Let me start with two vignettes from Proust, in this case from *A l'ombre des jeunes filles en fleurs*–"In the shadow of young girls in bloom"–the second volume of *In Search of Lost Time* (and rendered in English as *Within a Budding Grove*). The vignettes are but a few pages apart. Marcel has just seen the gaggle of the young girls in bloom, and there was one in particular who gave him a "smiling, sidelong glance, aimed from the centre of that inhuman world which enclosed the life of this little tribe, an inaccessible, unknown world wherein the idea of what I was could certainly never penetrate or find a place." He goes on:

> From the depths of what universe did she discern me? It would have been as difficult for me to say as, when certain distinguishing features in a neighbouring planet are made visible thanks to the telescope, it is to conclude therefrom that human beings inhabit it, and that they can see us, and to guess what ideas the sight of us can have aroused in their minds.

This wonder over who she is, writes Proust, leads Marcel to think:

And it was consequently her whole life that filled me with desire; a sorrowful desire because I felt that it was not to be fulfilled, but an exhilarating one because, what had hitherto been my life having ceased of a sudden to be my whole life, being no more now than a small part of the space stretching out before me which I was burning to cover and which was composed of the lives of these girls, it offered me that prolongation, that possible multiplication of oneself, which is happiness.

So happiness is the possibility of entering another world, or another culture, which will lead to a multiplication of oneself—an extension to greater realms. Two pages later, Marcel ruminates on the role of the imagination in this process:

To strip our pleasures of imagination is to reduce them to their own dimensions, that is to say to nothing....We need imagination, awakened by the uncertainty of being unable to attain its object, to create a goal which hides the other goal from us, and by substituting for sensual pleasures the idea of penetrating another life, prevents us from recognising that pleasure, from tasting its true savour, from restricting it to its own range.

By comparison, Proust imagines sitting before a plate of fish, and says that between us and the enjoyment of the flesh of that fish we need a certain intervention. We imagine sitting by the water with the rod in our hand, and see "the rippling eddy to whose surface come flashing... the bright gleam of flesh, the hint of a form, in the fluidity of a transparent and mobile azure." The imagination thus moves in to replace the actual sensual experience (whether of savoring a woman or a fish). This, he seems to suggest, is the Other World that we wish to enter, that offers happiness–the enlargement of oneself.

I remember an ad that was popular in the 1960s–it could have been for aftershave, for all I know–showing an elegantly dressed man sitting at a table surrounded by classic Japanese wood-and-paper screens (*shoji*), on which was a Go set. The caption read something like: "He is at home in worlds most people don't even know exist." And I remember, as a young adult, identifying with that man, wanting to be him, wanting familiarity with unknown worlds–probably because I understood that this would extend my own world, and thus make me happier.

The notion that the imaginary does *not* substitute for the sensual, but is somehow fused with it, is a major motif in the work of the great Japanese writer Jun'ichiro Tanizaki (1886-1965). In *Visions of Desire: Tanizaki's Fictional Worlds*, Ken Ito explores this in detail, showing how Tanizaki is able to create shimmering visions of other worlds–including the world of his childhood–which transcend the ordinary. As he puts it, "Tanizaki's other worlds are realms limned by culturally determined erotic longing, where men find sensual and aesthetic satisfactions unavailable in the given world of modernizing Japan."

In fact, in his early work, the West was the other world, the other culture, that Tanizaki found fascinating, and sought to enter. A bit later, he reversed himself, and made the lost traditional world of Japan, a world that was rapidly succumbing to modernization (i.e., Americanization), the culture that was alluring. After the War, Tanizaki came to a more integrated position, and broadened out to an examination of "the desire that underlies cultural aspiration" in general. He became, in short, both a brilliant psychologist and a brilliant storyteller, in a single stroke.

Tanizaki's novels, says Ito, "brim with characters who labor to realize visions of sexual and cultural fulfillment in the exterior world." *Naomi*, for example, is the story of a westernized Japanese woman who is the obsession of Joji, a Japanese man who cannot really distinguish between his yearning for her and his yearning for the West–at least, the West as it existed then in the popular Japanese imagination (powerful, sensual, and replete with all kinds of exotic possibilities). Similarly, in his description of his childhood, Tanizaki evokes "an 'other world' that transcends the ordinary," a world of mystery, in which "sampling just a bit of squid, salty and slick, can be a revelation; the way to a noodle shop can lead through a scene straight out of a Hiroshige print; and a restaurant's garden can take on the hazy luminosity of a 'dream world'." Treated in this way, even one's own childhood can be exotic. As one Japanese writer put it, in a commentary on Tanizaki, "exoticism is an attempt to find something lacking within the self in an object or person that is foreign, strange, or distant. It can thus be defined as an outwardly projected act of self-recovery."

(My own encounter with the fusion of sexuality and otherness occurred with my second sexual partner–I was lucky, I guess–who was half Native American. The sensation was something along the lines of, "Where have I been all my life?" For this went way beyond "getting laid"; it was an entrée into a world the existence of which I previously had no idea. Its dimensions seemed gigantic; I suddenly realized that Mystery was not just a concept, and that understood properly, the whole world could be experienced as erotic. Sad to say, that relationship didn't last very long, and it was more than ten years before it happened to me again. *C'est la vie.*)

This definition of exoticism has a lot in common with Georges Batailles' definition of eroticism, which he characterizes as a process where "man is everlastingly in search of an object *outside* himself but this object answers the *innerness* of the desire." Of course, the real question is whether it does answer the innerness of desire. The French psychologist, Jacques Lacan (1901-81), believed it didn't. For Lacan, these other worlds that we are reaching for, and the desire that impels us, are purely illusory. Lacan argued that the transference that occurs in the analytic situation is really to the knowledge that the patient thinks his or her analyst possesses. The analyst is the *sujet supposé savoir*, the subject who is supposedly in the know. But what Lacan occasionally hinted at, and what he actually demonstrated in his own life–in his consummate capacity as a charlatan–was that there *was* no hidden knowledge, no other world. As in the case of *The Wizard of Oz*, in which the various characters believe themselves to be incomplete (lacking a heart, a brain, etc.) and go off in search of the Wizard, who is supposedly going to make them whole, the journey ends when the "Wizard" turns out to be a nobody. He is just some little bald guy behind a screen, fiddling with levers and pulleys. The knowledge, the other world, was totally in the mind of the desirers. True fulfillment, true self-recovery, consists in grasping that the journey was completely unnecessary. Unfortunately, as Lacan well knew, very few people are willing to recognize this. For then the game would be up, and one would be faced with a very different, and much less dazzling, version of reality.

(I recall a joke in which a young American adventurer learns of some guru in the Himalayas who supposedly knows what life really is. He crosses the Atlantic, hitchhikes through Europe and Asia, climbs the Himalayas, and finally corners the guru, meditating in his cave. "Oh Swami!" he cries, "please tell me what life really is!" The guru, in an authoritative, high-pitched voice, points his finger toward the heavens and declares, "Life is a waterfall." The young lad stares at him for a moment and finally says, with some anger, "That's it? Life is a waterfall? I came all this way to hear that 'life is a waterfall'?" The guru looks at him, a bit puzzled, and then says: "It isn't?")

What, then, would be this less dazzling version of reality, and how does it relate to the theme of other worlds? One pioneer in this area–one might well call him the grandfather of body work–was F.M. Alexander (1869-1955), an Australian actor who immigrated to England in

1904 and subsequently developed a technique of mind-body integration that bears his name. He had some very famous students, including Aldous Huxley, who immortalized him as a seer and visionary (as "James Miller") in his novel, *Eyeless in Gaza*. Alexander was also in search of other worlds, and an expanded self, but in his hands (literally) these things took on a whole new meaning. For according to Alexander, it is precisely the refusal to indulge in desire, and to inhibit it instead, that opens up a new possibility. In his work with his clients, he sought to disrupt the well-worn grooves of habit and replace them with spontaneity. While not strictly ascetic, the lure here is that a much fuller life awaits one who does not act on impulse, but instead renounces it. This involves crossing a kind of watershed, of the kind I discuss in the final chapter of my book *Coming to Our Senses,* "The Two Faces of Creativity." I call these Creativity II and Creativity III, the first being allied to the tormented genius theory, fueled by drama and conflict–Van Gogh, let's say, or Sylvia Plath. The second is illustrated by the medieval craft tradition, or by much Eastern art, in which the work emerges out of serenity rather than emotional extremes. I point out that it is very hard for us westerners to get to Cr. III because the impulsive, passionate nature of Cr. II makes it seem so alive; and until you reach the other shore, the feeling is one of meaninglessness, loss of purpose. Those who study things such as the Alexander Technique, or emptiness meditation, eventually find themselves face to face with this "dark night of the soul."

In *The Compassionate Presence*, Stephen Schwartz talks in similar terms, ones which are reminiscent of my discussion of creativity. The first type, he says, is ego-driven and conflict-based; it prods us into acting, doing. We remain ignorant of the awareness "that there is another kind of impetus besides the motivation of 'should' and 'must'." This other impetus arises out of trust, not pressure, whereas "ego suggests that no challenge will exist when we stop pushing our life into the ground." However, if we let go of the old ways before we are ready for the new, Schwartz goes on to say, "a certain kind of forward-directed activity seems to cease." The ego sees the resulting deflation as "proof" of its theory, that drivenness is the key to life.

"We find ourselves for a while in a kind of paralysis," writes Schwartz. "This can feel like a barren place," a place of no hope. It's a half-way place. "We find ourselves [there] because a specific kind of certainty does not yet exist in full consciousness." But eventually, another kind of impulse arises, one that is not the result of pushing and doubt. Proust (let alone the Buddha) would say that very few of us get there. In Tolstoy's famous story of Ivan Ilych, the central character–Everyman, in a word–realizes only on his deathbed that his entire life was a waste of time.

This is where Alexander is relevant, for his teaching was designed to help people work through this "dark night of the soul" on a bodily level. It means putting yourself in physical postures that seem wrong only because you've been doing what's wrong all your life. As in the case of Wilhelm Reich, the idea is to return to a "natural" body, one without tension, without the coercive ego structure of pushing and doubt. "If it feels wrong, leave it wrong," Alexander used to tell his students. The entire process of the Alexander Technique is counterintuitive. In this case, the other world is an inner rather than an outer world, and as already noted, it is attained not through desire but through its inhibition. This has obvious connections with Buddhism or Taoism, and the classical Chinese notion of *wu wei*, or not-doing. The promise is that of a richer existence, a happiness borne not out of the multiplication of self, but out of the holding back of the self. As someone once said, Zen is the practice of manifesting oneself as emptiness. The paradox is that renunciation creates a sensation of fullness, of limitless horizons.

Similar conclusions were reached independently by the Polish psychiatrist Kazimierz Dabrowski (1902-80), who pioneered something called the Theory of Positive Disintegration. Dabrowski saw depression and anxiety as necessary for real growth, disintegrative processes that he regarded as positive because they were developmental. Crises, in other words, cause us to review ourselves, possibly redo ourselves, and to make new worlds as a result. One has to weather the darkness, which is not conceived of in negative terms. (Not easy!)

I have repeated this cycle of drivenness/surrender a number of times in my life, most recently in the wake of surgery that left me confined to my house for a few weeks. My doctor told me the following were off limits: spicy foods, fats, sugar, salt, soda pop, tobacco, coffee, too much food in general, sex, exercise, and driving anywhere. After three weeks of this, I was pretty much a basket case. It was as though all my "friends" had suddenly deserted me. I had no interest in doing any work; indeed, it felt like nothing would ever turn me on again. Finally, as Dabrowski says, one has no choice (in lieu of spiraling downward) but to trust the process, give it a positive "spin". In time, with a little luck (or maybe it's divine intervention, who knows), the outlines of the farther shore emerge, and one lives to write, and love, again.

16. Ways of Knowing

There are a few books one encounters in the course of one's life that prove to be transformative. In most cases, one is not expecting this. But it happens, and you know that you'll never look at the world in quite the same way. For me, one text that was particularly life-changing was a slender volume by the classical scholar John Finley, entitled *Four Stages of Greek Thought*. It was as if, within its pages, I discovered what kind of writer I wanted to be; even, what kind of life I wanted to lead.

Finley distinguishes between the heroic-visionary world of the Homeric Greeks and the theoretical-rational world of their successors. There is a scene in the *Iliad*, he tells us, in which Hector briefly leaves the battlefield and returns to Troy, to visit his wife and infant son. Standing in front of his house, he reaches out to take the child in his arms, but the boy draws back, frightened at Hector's helmet with its horsehair crest. Hector laughs, takes off the helmet, and puts it down; and Homer then records how the helmet sits there on the ground, all shiny and motionless, reflecting the light of the sun. The Homeric world, says Finley, is one of brilliant particulars, fixed entities that are what they are, nothing more or less. It is not an especially comforting world, he tells us, but it is at least this: absolutely clear. "Happiness, one sometimes thinks, is clarity of vision, moments when things stand clear in sharpest outline...as if revealed for the first time." He goes on: "However intoxicating the attractions of intellect, and however essential to the structures by which we live, something in us wants also the clear signals of the senses by which alone the world is made fresh and definite."

This is, I suppose, the world of childhood, made magical by its very realism; and there certainly is something intoxicating about it: the wind in one's hair, the shock of a cool lake on a warm summer's day, the dry texture of an autumn leaf. Yet Finley uses the word "intoxicating" not to refer to the world of sensual immediacy, but to that of the intellect, which has its own siren song. Once we enter the world of Socrates and Plato, and the "sunlit tangibility of the fourth century" (fine phrase, that), there is no going back. The experience of rationality, of *conceptual* clarity, is so overwhelming that once "infected," the mind will settle for nothing less. When Archimedes (allegedly) cried "Eureka!" in his bathtub, his excitement was over having discovered a *pattern* (in this case, the law of specific gravity), not over the sensual impact of the water on his skin.

This issue of pattern is the key to the phenomenon of intellectual intoxication, and probably first occurs, in a formal sense, in the work of Plato. "Noetic" understanding, the job of the philosopher-king, moves along a vertical line, upwards toward the gods. Indeed, it is widely accepted that this vertical model is based on the shamanic or revealed knowledge of the Mystery Religions that were popular in ancient Greece. One application of it can be seen in Plato's *Republic*, in the famous "parable of the cave," in which people sit with their backs to the light and take the shadows cast on the wall for reality. Such individuals are asleep, says Plato, whereas the true philosopher, the one who is awake, turns to the light, the actual source of the perceived phenomena. What you see, then, is not what you get; real knowledge requires this type of "vertical" understanding, this digging beneath the surface. It is not for nothing that Freud compared his own analytical method to the science of archaeology. (Indeed, Heinrich Schliemann was digging up the ruins of Troy during Freud's lifetime.) What is on the surface, for Freud, is social behavior; what lies underneath this is repressed sexuality (hence the title of one of his most famous books, *The Psychopathology of Everyday Life*). In the case of Marx, the surface consists of class relations; the reality, the underlying pattern, is the mode of production of a society at any given stage in its history. For Gassendi, Descartes, and Newton, gross objects were mere appearances; the reality was atomic particles. A sunset may be beautiful, but the "truth" of the situation is refracted light. And so on. Cognition of this sort can hit you with the force of a hurricane.

The alternative mode of knowing is more "horizontal": what you see is what you get. Or as Wittgenstein once put it, "depths are on the surface." The whole phenomenological school—I am thinking of Husserl and Merleau-Ponty in particular—argues for direct physical experience as the key to the world (the sun gleaming off of Hector's helmet, for example). The power of this type of understanding derives from the sheer "is-ness" of things, their pure ontology. To "know" a sunset as refracted light may be to not know it at all.

My oldest friend and I discovered, soon after we met, that we shared the same dilemma: we were torn between these two worlds. Both of them were intoxicating, in their own special way; so much so that we found it impossible to give either of them up. His solution was to create two separate, consecutive lives. Thus he spent three decades as a professional scientist, after which he retired to devote himself to photography, yoga, and jazz piano. My solution was to try to bring the two worlds together, and it cost me dearly. No university department could figure out what the hell I was doing, and typically regarded my writing as weird. In a culture severely split between mind and body, I could only be regarded as some sort of "cult figure," at best. And really, what else could I expect? If you are going to insist that the dominant culture is ontologically crippled, it is not likely that that culture is going to stand up and cheer.

Reading Finley, in any case, provided me with a keen sense of validation, because he doesn't end his analysis with a description of the two worlds and leave it at that. The "character of a great age," he writes, is when the two worlds come together, and when, as a result, "meanings seem within people's reach." According to him, this unity found its greatest expression in Greece in the fifth century B.C., somewhere between Homer and Aristotle:

> Part of the grip on the imagination that fifth-century Athens never ceases to hold is that these two kinds of worlds met then, the former culminating as the latter came into being. Aeschylus and Sopho-

cles spoke for the older outlook that saw things through shape; Socrates and Thucydides for the nascent mind that saw them through idea.

It seems unlikely that we shall ever have such an age again, though who knows what the world will be like five hundred years hence. For now, at least, the integration of mind and body will probably remain a private experience: the intellect that feels, the sensuality that thinks. But ultimately, the commitment of the writer, or of anyone invested in the world of letters, the larger culture, cannot be restricted to individual experience, for solipsism is not an answer to anything. Putting meaning "within people's reach" is finally what it is all about.

17. Is There Life After Birth? A Review of *Abel*, by Diego Luna

It is generally accepted that the author of any creative work is only half conscious of what he or she is doing. Indeed, without this sort of "vagueness," or indeterminacy, multiple interpretations of a novel, poem, or screenplay—which are the norm—would not be possible. And if the author objects, says, "but that's not what I meant," it isn't completely arrogant for the critic to reply, "no—at least not consciously." So let me put aside any false modesty here and say what I think this strange and remarkable film is "really" about.

Although it is not as popular today as it was forty years ago (give or take), there is a mode of treating psychological disturbances known as "family systems therapy," in which the therapist regards the pathology displayed by an individual as symptomatic of a larger problem—usually, a secret—that is woven into the fabric of the person's familial relationships. Within the family, there is an unspoken agreement that this thing, whatever it is, will never be mentioned. What the supposedly disturbed individual—say, a sixteen-year-old boy—is trying to do when he steals a car and gets caught, is bring attention to the family secret; to flush it out. (In psychological jargon this is called "acting out.") Therapy that focuses only on the adolescent and his criminal activity—makes him the "Identified Patient," so to speak—is missing the boat, on this interpretation. In truth, the kid is a healing agent, trying to expose the rot in the system, if only the family would be willing to stop playing an elaborate game of self-deception. In fact, if the son cleans up his act, stops stealing cars, and starts getting good grades in school, what happens? The fifteen-year-old daughter, previously a paragon of virtue, suddenly shows up pregnant. If she has the baby, gives it up for adoption, stops sleeping around, and manages to work out a healthy adolescent life, the father, amazingly enough, starts to drink. If he then goes to Alcoholics Anonymous and quits drinking, the mother becomes schizophrenic and is committed to a mental institution. Or perhaps hangs herself. You get the idea. The one thing the family does not want to do is address the Big Secret, the pathology that lies underneath the pathology. So like Hegel's *zeitgeist,* the ghost, the energy, keeps moving from person to person, making it look as though each successive "Identified Patient" is the problem, when it is actually the family dynamic that is the real problem.

In many ways, *Abel* is a quintessentially Mexican film. As a foreigner who has lived in Mexico for four years now, and has been visiting the place for more than thirty, I have been acutely aware of the juxtaposition of socioeconomic poverty and sensual intensity. In keeping with this, the action of the film takes place in a shabby, rundown area of an unnamed city (in fact, Aguascalientes), and this contrasts sharply with the exquisite photography of the film, which gives the movie an incredible texture, at once tactile and visual. But beyond that, the theme seems universal, for the story can very well be analyzed in terms of family systems therapy. In fact, what came to mind for me when I was watching it was a British tale of family dysfunction written around four hundred years ago—*King Lear*, by William Shakespeare—and a short story written nearly fifty years ago by the Israeli writer A.B. Yehoshua, "Facing the Forests." In all three of these works—the film, the play, the story—the Identified Patient is depressed/autistic (the child in *Abel*), supposedly mad (the Fool in *Lear*), or unable to speak (an old Arab who had his tongue cut out). In each case, their particular version of silence is witness to the Big Secret, and represents it metaphorically.

Lear

Interested in flattery, the king commits a fatal error, believing the false declarations of love given to him by his two eldest daughters, Goneril and Regan, and failing to realize that it is his youngest, Cordelia, who really loves him for who he is. Worse, he disowns her for *not* flattering him. Meanwhile, the Fool keeps babbling his "nonsense," which is actually insight into what is really going on, if only Lear would listen. Instead, the king eventually goes mad; at that point, the Fool disappears—he is no longer needed. But had Lear come to terms with the Big Secret, confronted the family dynamic, the Fool would not have been needed in the first place, and the insanity never have happened. (Also, there would have been no play!) Unfortunately, as any family systems therapist can tell you, health is the rare exception to the rule, which can be summarized as, "Let the charade continue!"

Facing the Forests

Here, the "family" is Israel/Palestine, and the "therapist" is the author of the story, who is trying to heal his society. Yehoshua's novella is about a graduate student in history who takes a job with the forest service, his assignment being to guard against forest fires. The forest consists of trees planted since 1948 to celebrate the state of Israel, most of them being paid for by American Jews. The family mythology, which is partly true, is one of pioneers in a new land, Holocaust survivors determined to make the Zionist dream a reality. The Big Secret is that in the process of doing that, 700,000 Palestinian Arabs, some deliberately and some as an accidental by-product of war, were forced to flee their homes and their land. In Yehoshua's story (and in reality as well, on more than one occasion), an Arab village was bulldozed to make way for the newly planted forest of pine trees. Flitting between the slender pines, a sort of caretaker and his daughter inhabit the premises, haunt them, one might say, like ghosts. But as I already indicated, the old Arab cannot speak—he was apparently tortured, had his tongue cut out. With a little research, the history student pieces together what happened to the village, and manages to communicate with the old Arab about it through gestures. By this time, however, the Arab has had it, and burns down the forest in revenge. The police arrest him and interrogate him, asking him the same questions over and over again, and the student says to himself: "A foul stench rises from the burnt forest, as though a huge carcass were rotting away all around them. The interrogation gains momentum. A big bore. What did he see, what did he hear, what did he do. It's insulting, this insistence upon the tangible—as though that were the main point, as though there weren't some idea involved here."

But the student remains silent. Neither he nor anybody else is going to say out loud what the main point, the large, intangible idea, is, because to do that would blow the lid on the family mythology. Instead of dealing with its past, and the Big Secret, Israel prefers to symbolically make this old Arab without a voice the Identified Patient. That was in 1963, a mere fifteen years after the War of Independence (or the Catastrophe, if you are talking to an Arab). Nearly fifty years later, and despite a growing literature by a number of very talented revisionist historians, the majority of Israelis (judging from how they have voted in recent elections) still can't seem to fathom the violence and "rebelliousness" of these "wayward" Palestinian "children," who could solve the whole problem of the Middle East if they just "behaved themselves" and stopped acting "irrationally." (I've actually heard Israelis talk in these terms.) Yehoshua was trying to shine some light on the Big Secret, but this is largely taboo in Israeli society, and certainly was in 1963. For the most part, then, the charade continues.

Abel

On to the film. The plot is something like this: Two years ago, Anselmo, the father in this particular family drama, declared he was going to the U.S. to work, and left. His eight-year-old son, Abel, went into a deep depression as a result and had to be hospitalized. Two years later, his doctor believes he is ready to come home, even though he displays the characteristics of an autistic child. So he returns home, and everyone—mother, sister, brother—sort of walks on eggshells around him, as the doctor has indicated that Abel is not to be upset in any way. The problem is that his behavior becomes increasingly erratic, as he seems to think he is the father of the family and to act accordingly. He puts a ring on his mother's finger, and starts sleeping in her bed. He wears his father's clothes. He also "drops" his autism and begins to talk, mostly giving orders to the other members of the family. He signs his sister's report card from school, and checks her homework. Rather creepy, but everyone plays along with it.

Out of the blue, Anselmo comes back home; but before he can re-assert his role as father, Cecilia, Abel's mother, tells the child that this is her cousin. Soon Anselmo is playing along with this farce as well, even though he (rightly) regards the situation as nuts. By chance, the daughter examines the photographs in her father's digital camera, only to discover that he has another wife (or perhaps it is a girlfriend) and a child by her. It turns out he was only in the United States for two months; the rest of the time he was living a completely separate family life some distance away in the town of Saltillo. One night during this time, i.e. the time of Anselmo's return, Abel climbs on top of his mother and pretends he is having sex with her, then pretends to smoke a post-coital cigarette. The next morning he announces to the family that he and Cecilia have had sex, and that she is pregnant. For Anselmo, this is the last straw, and he confronts Abel with the fact that he is his father. Abel spins out of control and deliberately injures himself; in general, all hell breaks loose. Undaunted, Anselmo finds Abel's doctor and signs him back into the hospital in Mexico City. We then see Anselmo in his truck on the road back to Saltillo, abandoning the family once again, and Cecilia visiting Abel in the hospital, where he is emotionally vacant and has returned to his autistic behavior.

What in the world?

If we try to decode this bizarre tale by means of family systems therapy, it seems fairly obvious that the family mythology in this case is that there actually is a family. But the truth, the Big Secret, is that the father has another family, and doesn't really give a damn about this one. He returns momentarily, and claims to be the father of this family, which he is biologically; but the truth is that he has no legitimacy. On some level, Abel knows all this, in the uncanny way that children typically do. And so, in a parody of the family lie, he takes over the function of the father. He is not quite acting; he really seems to believe it. And yet it is a charade, one that has two crucial systemic functions. First, it cancels out the abandonment: if the family now has a father, even if it is Abel himself, then Abel has not been abandoned and in fact feels (and acts) healthy and strong, for his world has been sewn back together. He is alive as the "father," dead as the abandoned son. Second, as the Identified Patient, Abel is unconsciously trying to send a signal to the family that this situation is fucked up beyond belief; in a word, he's trying to repair the mess in some weird sort of way. Yet the family dynamic, as before, is to pretend that nothing is amiss, or more precisely, that it is only Abel that is the problem. The "crazy" behavior of the child is in fact a type of intuitive wisdom, for it is the entire situation that is crazy. Focusing on Abel's apparent insanity, and not willing (or able) to admit that if anyone precipitated this situation it was himself, Anselmo blows the whistle and has Abel sent back to the hospital. And then, asshole that he is, he abandons the boy, and the family, as he did two years before. So this "solution" solves nothing, because the Big Secret, the fact that this family is in no way a family, never gets dealt with. Thus we are back to Square One, with Anselmo having gone AWOL and the kid in the hospital, once again emotionally dead. As in the case of the hypothetical family I described earlier, or the family of King Lear, or the "family" of Israel/Palestine, the temptation to focus on the Identified Patient rather than get to the heart of the matter is too powerful to resist, because getting to the heart of the matter is inevitably terrifying. Not to put too fine a point on it, *Abel* is nothing less than a work of genius. It is at once a Mexican tragedy, a Shakespearean tragedy, a Middle Eastern tragedy, and a universal tragedy, which can be summarized in the words of the British poet W.H. Auden: "We would rather be ruined than changed." Great stories generally don't have happy endings, what can I tell you.

18. Be Here Now

I often wonder how many people in their sixties or seventies have had this experience: you awake one morning and realize that forty years went by in the blink of an eye. You can barely remember them; it all seems like one big blur. What stands out is the suddenness of this passage of time. One day you were a young adult, and the next day (seemingly) you are a Senior Citizen. What in the world? you ask yourself. Where *was* I all that time?

As Proust told us, the past can only be recaptured kinesthetically, as a somatic memory that is largely fragmentary in nature. Much of this is intertwined with desire. But since desire pursues a "moving target," so to speak, our personal history seems like an illusion, or even a hallucination. It is for this reason that the fantasy of wanting to return to an earlier point in our lives and "do it over again," but with our present adult consciousness intact, is a common one—the subject of a number of films, in fact.

All this has led me to think of how I might avoid repeating this feeling that I wasn't present for most of my life. Proust's solution to this conundrum was what he called "intermittence"—submission to the "great turning wheel of experience." It has an obvious affinity with the Buddhist concept of awareness. But it poses certain problems. First, how can I get myself to be aware of my experience as I am having it? It seems more likely that I shall forget to remember. Second, even if I were to become successful at doing this, there is no guarantee that on my deathbed, I won't experience the past twenty or thirty years, once again, as a blur that went by like a speeding train. Either way, life will have passed me by.

Recently, motivated by some odd form of nostalgia, I searched the Internet for my first love, the girl I dated during my sophomore year in college. Much to my surprise, I found her: she was a successful architect, living in a small town in Virginia. Ironically enough, I had worked in that very town for several years; she and I probably passed each other on the street, or sat in the same cafés together without realizing it. The picture that came up on the screen, of a woman in her early sixties, confronted me with a parallel universe, as it were: had things "worked out," this person could have been my life. Not that I had any regrets, or sadly missed that alternative possibility; but that she had floated out of my life, only to reappear as a virtual image forty-five years later, was a weird sensation. I thought of writing her, but finally decided against it. What did we really have to say to one another, after all this time? That relationship was someone else's life.

Truth be told, I have found my "actual" life to be not very different from my dream life. I recall one dream I had when I was thirty...I was taking a bus to a different city, ostensibly to begin a new life, and, having gotten on the bus, discovered that my luggage was sitting out on the curb. I told the driver I needed to get it before we took off, but he told me that as this was a Sunday, the rule (for some strange reason) was that I had to travel without it or not at all. While I was trying to decide what to do, I looked just behind the area where the bus driver was sitting, and noticed a large circular badge or button, made out of metal, on which the words were written, in Spanish, "Doctor of Bone Medicine Aboard." (This was particularly odd, because at that point in my life, I knew practically no Spanish.) I told the bus driver I would stay on the bus, and leave my baggage behind; whereupon he started the engine, and the bus left the station.

When I awoke, I had the feeling that the message in Spanish was related to a then-popular tune by Paul Simon, "Everything Put Together Falls Apart." "Paraphernalia," says the song, can't hide your broken bones. One thing that I felt the dream was telling me was that in order to undertake a journey of freedom, of unfolding consciousness, I had to leave my emotional "baggage" behind. The second message seemed equally clear: nobody could heal me but myself; *I* was the "Doctor of Bone Medicine" accompanying myself on this journey. *I* would mend my broken bones, and I would not use paraphernalia (gimmicks or substitute satisfactions) to do it. And finally, the notion that life was fleeting, impermanent. We want things to last, but they don't.

Some years later, I ran across a poem by Juan Ramón Jiménez that seemed to echo this existential reality (my translation):

I am not I.
I am this one
who walks beside me, without my seeing him

whom I sometimes see
and whom I sometimes forget.
Who is quiet, serene, when I talk
who forgives me, gently, when I hate
who walks where I am not
who will remain standing when I die.

Perhaps this is the "intermittence" that Proust was referring to; I'm not sure.

In any case, I find myself thinking about death a lot these days, and wondering what that will be like. Since I don't believe in an afterlife, I imagine it as a letting go into nothingness–not a pleasant prospect. The Zen idea of being fully present in every experience doesn't have much attraction for me, in this case, and I always admired the total honesty and simplicity of Zen master Shunryu Suzuki's last words: "I don't want to die." When all is said and done, none of us escapes the human condition.

Last words, of course, say a lot about the person who utters them. "Tell them I've had a wonderful life," said Wittgenstein, as he slipped out of consciousness and into the Great Void. I can't imagine I'll enjoy the same peace of mind. My guess is it will be more like, "You mean, this is it?" All those fragments–the girl I dated in college and found decades later on the Net, the dream about the "Bone Doctor," the time I was seven years old and sat on the beach at Lake Ontario, playing in the sand with a pail and shovel–what, finally, did it all mean? Quite obviously, there is no forcing things to make sense: either they do or they don't, and there is no guarantee that they will.

I recall, in 1973, visiting Prague (I was living in London at the time), and being politely accosted, in English, by an elderly Czech gentleman sitting on a bench on a street just off Wenceslas Square. He was wearing a suit, overcoat, and hat, and explained to me that he often hung out in the touristy sections of the city so that he might get a chance to practice his foreign language skills–French, Russian, German, English. His name–I remember it to this day–was Jan Horna, and there was something very dignified about him, very self-contained. We chatted for about half an hour, after which I asked him if I might take his photograph. He agreed, on condition that I write down his address and send him a copy of the photo; which I subsequently did. The picture captured him exactly, sitting on the bench with a look that was both wistful and questioning. I assume he is long gone by now, buried in some cemetery in Prague. I think about him from time to time, and wonder how the rest of his life turned out.

19. Fate

One film I keep returning to—I must have seen it at least five or six times now—is *Damage*, by Louis Malle. The story is a kind of Greek tragedy. Jeremy Irons plays a successful British civil servant whose inner life is empty; Juliette Binoche is his son's fiancé, with whom he gets involved immediately after they meet. By chance, his son comes to the flat where they are having a tryst, and catches them in bed. Thunderstruck, the young man backs out of the room and falls backward over the banister, plunging several stories down the center of the apartment building to his death.

His life thus destroyed, the man retires from the world. He takes up residence in a small town in an unidentified country, perhaps Greece or Italy. Life consists of shopping, cooking, and washing up, along with spending entire days sitting in front of a blown-up photograph of the fateful triangle—himself, his son, and the girl—which is mounted on the wall. He has, in effect, constructed some sort of shrine; but to what?

The man ponders what happened to him—events that were (or seem to have been) completely out of his control. He never knew who the woman really was, and yet the attachment went way beyond sex. As a high-level bureaucrat, he experienced his life as totally meaningless. He gave TV interviews and public speeches that were perfectly turned out—he said all the right things—but in reality, he was a shell. The girl, for some unknown reason, promised to fill that void (or so he believed, on an unconscious level), and so the chemistry was instantaneous, ferocious. Now, in the aftermath of it all, the man spends his time staring at the photograph, trying to decipher what it all meant.

What makes us, he says to himself, is beyond knowing. We surrender to love because it gives us some sense of what is unknowable. Nothing else matters, not in the end. I saw her only one more time, at an airport while changing planes. She didn't see me. She was with a man, and carrying a child in her arms. She was no different from anyone else.*

She was no different from anyone else. This realization—perhaps only momentary—means that the "shrine" was not dedicated to the woman, nor even to the love that they shared, but to love itself. But perhaps much more than that. The purpose of the shrine, the need for it, is to worship that thing that is beyond knowing, the only thing that matters in the end. So what is it?

If human life is finally a mystery, the key in the lock is not that hard to figure out: it's the sense of a Presence larger than oneself, and beyond the grasp of the rational intellect. For hunter-gatherers, this was a presence with a small "p": their reality was immanent, was the environment itself. (The "great spirit" of the Plains Indians was typically the wind.) With agricultural civilization and the rise of religion, the Presence became transcendent, exalted to a "vertical" reality: God. Yet this presence, or Presence–this irreducible otherness–is finally within *us*. In

Damage, the central character projects this "divinity" onto a perfectly ordinary person, which he comes to understand only years later. Yet the photo remains on the wall, and the daily "worship" remains the central activity of his life. Love gives us some sense of the unknowable, and the unknowable—even though it arises as an interaction between the self and the outer world—is unfathomable, as is the interaction. Hence, the enormous fascination, born out of the conviction people have that the experience embodies some great truth; which it does. Yet no amount of analysis or contemplation can resolve it; it just is.

Damage can be framed in many ways. I have already referred to Greek tragedy, but we can see it through the lens of Christian allegory as well. We have a man—say, Saul of Tarsus—going through the motions of a meaningless, ritualistic life. Suddenly, he is blinded on the road to Damascus, and that vision, or apparition, redefines his reality. In so doing, it tears up the old life, lifts him on transcendent wings, and finally deposits him in a chair in front of a photograph, bathed in the light of Christ. It's not likely that the central character of *Damage*, even beyond the death of his son, would ultimately have it any other way. After all, he went from No Meaning to Total Meaning—not exactly a trivial adventure. As he says to himself at the end, as he walks the streets of his new home, "I found a life that was my own." Who of us doesn't want that?

Of course, much of a political nature could be added at this point. Mesmerization by the cross, no less than by the swastika or the hammer and sickle (to name but a few), has caused many millions of deaths. This is just a matter of historical fact, and I don't mean to treat it lightly. But it seems to me that it has a larger context, an anthropological one: namely, that the need to feel a part of something greater–even if immanent, as in the case of hunter-gatherers–has been with us for at least 100,000 years, when the first light of self-conscious awareness glimmered in the brain of Cro-Magnon Man. The birth of the self, in a word, may have been coincident with the desire to immerse the self, and thereby to endow it with meaning. This is the very essence of *Homo sapiens sapiens*, and it is not likely to leave us any time soon.

Viewed from this perspective, the "damage" of human relations, if not quite forgivable, is at least explicable. How much of our lives is driven by this archaic impulse? A good bit of it, I would guess; maybe even most of it. It is tempting to say, of course, that the solution is then fairly obvious: we have to get a "handle" on this impulse, to channel or control it in some way. This is the path (ideally, at least) of organized religion or psychoanalysis, and it is not completely in error. But it does tend to omit the central point, that of the need to *experience* the phenomenon–to be "taken" by life, to let life "come and get you" and make of you what it will, so that you might get washed up on the shore of some small town, staring at a picture on the wall–if that should happen to be your fate.

How many of us are willing to take that chance?

*This text does not occur in the novel by Josephine Hart, on which the film is based, but in the screenplay of the movie, by David Hare.

PART III
PROGRESS
TRUE AND
FALSE

20. The Moral Order

The notion that there was a way of life characteristic of modern (or industrial) societies that was qualitatively different from the way of life found in pre-modern (or folk) societies goes back, at least, to the German sociologist Max Weber. Modern societies, said Weber, were governed by bureaucracy; the dominant ethos was one of "rationalization," whereby everything was mechanized, administered according to the dictates of scientific reason. Weber famously compared this situation to that of an "iron cage": there was no way the citizens of these societies could break free from their constraints. Pre-modern societies, on the other hand, were permeated by animism, by a belief in magic and spirits, and governance came not through bureaucracy but through the charisma of gifted leaders. The decline of magic that accompanied the transition to modernity Weber called *die Entzauberung der Welt*–the disenchantment of the world.

The distinction between these two fundamental types of social orders emerged in a variety of contexts in the decades that followed. Thus Ferdinand Tönnies saw the two in terms of *Gemeinschaft* (community) vs. *Gesellschaft* (society, especially the culture of business), noting that whereas the former was characterized by bonds of kinship or friendship, the latter was notable for the preponderance of impersonal or contractual relations. Linguist Edward Sapir, in turn, cast the dichotomy in terms of "genuine" vs. "spurious" cultures, and eventually the American anthropologist Robert Redfield would label it the "moral vs. the technical order." In one of his last books, *The Primitive World and Its Transformations*, Redfield tried to argue that the technical order would eventually give rise to a new moral order; but it was finally not very convincing. Ultimately, Redfield believed that while the human race had made great advances in the technical order, it had made virtually no progress in the moral order—the knowledge of how to live, as it were—and that because of this, the human prospect was rather dim.

Indeed, for all one can say about the scientific inaccuracy of the pre-modern world, at least it was imbued with meaning. This is not the case with the modern industrial-corporate-consumer state, which expands technologically and economically, but to no other end than expansion itself. As the sociologist Georg Simmel wrote over a century ago, if you make money the center of your value system, then finally you *have* no value system, because money is not a value. All of these writers (a list that includes Franz Boas, Arthur Koestler, Jacques Ellul, and Lewis Mumford, *inter alia*) were pessimistic because they could see no way of reversing the direction of historical development. It was obvious that as time went on, the technical order was not merely overtaking the moral order, but actually obliterating it. This loss of meaning does much to account for the rise of the secular-religious movements of the twentieth century, including Communism, Fascism, Existentialism, Postmodernism, and so on. It also accounts for the depth and extent of <u>fundamentalist Christianity</u> in the United States. For there is no real meaning in the corporate-consumer state, which is at once empty and idiotic. On some level, everybody knows this.

We might, then, characterize the crashes of 1929 and 2008 as spiritual rather than strictly economic in nature. John Maynard Keynes saw the fluctuations of the stock market as being governed by human psychology, i.e. by faith and fear. So while in the case of both crashes, one can point to financial "bubbles" and hyperinflated investments, the core of meaninglessness at the center of the consumer-driven economy means that a boom-and-bust cycle is inevitable. In the case of the Depression, it took a war–which involved a huge mobilization of Meaning– to pull us out of it. At the present time, the situation is very different: American wars are now neo-colonial and self-destructive, a drain on the economy. They can only make the situation worse. Hence, the U.S. government has turned to massive bailouts of financial institutions as a solution, but this is analogous to putting band aids on the body of a cancer patient: the core of the problem remains untouched.

And what *is* the core of the problem? Basically, that the technical order is meaningless; that the American Way of Life finally has no moral center. Indeed, it is not clear that it ever did. In *Freedom Just Around the Corner*, historian Walter McDougall characterizes the United States as a "nation of hustlers," going back to its earliest days. What began as trade and opportunism finally issued out into a full-blown crisis of meaning, and it is this that now constitutes the crisis of late capitalism.

It is with this understanding that the political scientist Benjamin Barber published an article in *The Nation* some time ago (9 February 2009), claiming that the only thing that could save us was "a revolution in spirit." Barber points out that President Obama's economic advisory team (which includes Timothy Geithner and Lawrence Summers) is squarely in the tradition of neoliberalism and the corporate state. How, then, can we possibly expect the "change that makes a difference" that Obama promised the American people during his presidential campaign? As Barber notes, "it is hard to discern any movement toward a wholesale rethinking of the dominant role of the market in our society. No one is questioning the impulse to rehabilitate the consumer market as the driver of American commerce." His solution is to "refashion the cultural ethos" by shifting our values from shopping to the life of the mind. We need, he says, a new cabinet post for the arts and humanities, which will somehow get Americans to think in terms of creativity and the imagination, not in terms of mindless consumerism. "Imagine," writes Barber, "all the things we could do without having to shop: play and pray, create and relate, read and walk, listen and procreate—make art, make friends, make homes, make love." "Idealism," he concludes, "must become the new realism."

How is this change going to happen? What are the political forces that will bring it about? Barber doesn't say, and I confess that when I read his article, I couldn't help wondering if the man had suffered some kind of mental lapse. What also came to mind was a book written in 1977 by the American sociologist John Robinson, entitled *How Americans Use Time*. Robinson discovered that on an average daily basis, five minutes were spent on reading books (of any kind), one minute on making music, thirty seconds attending theater and concerts, and less than thirty seconds on visits to art galleries or museums. As depressing as these figures are, they are surely much worse thirty-odd years later, given the heavy corporatization of the culture, the dramatic increase in the attention paid to television and video screens in general, and the widely acknowledged decay of the American educational system. Indeed, the square footage of shopping malls in the United States—4 billion as of twelve years ago—vastly exceeds that of schools and churches. All of the available data show that the typical American citizen has about as much interest in the life of the mind as your average armadillo. Rather than being on the verge of some possible cultural renaissance, or a reversal of our entire history, what we are now witnessing is the slow-motion suicide of the nation, with Mr. Obama guiding us, in a genteel and semi-conscious way, into the grave. Indeed, what more can he, or anybody, do at this point? For despite appearances to the contrary, Professor Barber must know that substantive political change is not a matter of voluntarism or exhortatory messages or a purported cabinet post in the arts. These are little more than jokes. To buck 200-plus years of history requires massive political power moving in the opposite direction, and no such force has emerged on the horizon.

Nor will it. There is no record of a dying civilization reassessing its values (or lack of values, in our case) and altering its trajectory. Whether the type of moral order that Professor Barber has in mind actually exists, or might someday exist somewhere on the planet, is certainly worth debating. But what is *not* worth debating is whether such a moral order might make an appearance on American soil. History is about many things, but one thing it is not about is miracles.

21. How Chic Was My Progress

> When it was hip to be hep, I was hep.
> —From "I'm Hip," by Dave Frishberg and Bob Dorough

At one point in _The Labyrinth of Solitude,_ Octavio Paz quotes the German philosopher Max Scheler, who asked, "What is progress?" It's a crucial question, and in the United States there is basically only one answer, involving the visible expression of technological innovation and economic expansion. Paz was not impressed with this notion of progress in 1950, when he wrote his famous essay, and it is a safe bet that he was increasingly disenchanted with the American model as the years wore on. Although he saw the flaws of his own culture quite clearly, he never felt that the American Way of Life was any kind of solution for Mexico or indeed, the rest of the world. Paz was prescient: at a time when everyone was celebrating America as an unrivaled success, he correctly pegged it as a wounded civilization, one that saw the future strictly in terms of novelty and never questioned what it was doing.

This extremely limited notion of the good life, combined with almost total unconsciousness, presents itself as daily reality in the United States. I recall a friend of mine telling me, a few years ago, about a train trip she took up the California coast, during which she decided to walk through the cars very slowly, from back to front, almost pretending to be an invalid, so that she could eavesdrop on conversations. Every last one of these, she said, was about some gadget, some aspect of consumer technology—soft-

ᴏmputer attachments, iPods, cell phone variations, ᴛhis is where, she concluded, Americans put their ᴀᴛᴛᴇntion; it is what really excites them, makes them feel alive. Nor is this limited to Americans, of course. In the mid-eighties, when I was teaching at a Canadian university, my colleagues were literally ecstatic over the introduction of personal computers, firmly believing that these machines would write papers and books for them, perhaps help them get tenure or upgrade their entire careers (promises that failed to materialize, needless to say). As for south of the border, I was recently riding around Mexico City with a colleague of mine when we saw a huge billboard ad for some cell phone, with the caption, in three-foot high block capitals (in English, for some strange reason), KILL SILENCE. "Well," I remarked to my colleague, "at least they are being honest about it." "Oh," he quipped, "you are fixated on technology."

It's hard to know how to reply to a dismissive remark of this kind, since even the brightest people don't get it, and usually have no idea what George Steiner meant when he called modernity "the systematic suppression of silence." Silence, after all, is the source of all self-knowledge, and of much creativity as well. But it is hardly valued by societies that confuse creativity with productivity, and incessant noise with aliveness. What I am fixated on, in fact, is not technology but the *fixation* on technology, the obsession with it. Unfortunately, it is hard to persuade those caught up in the American model of progress that it is they who are living in an upside-down world, not Octavio Paz.

One way to see this, perhaps, is in terms of a traditional religious framework. In _A Book of Silence_, Sara Maitland writes:

> In the Middle Ages Christian scholastics argued that the devil's basic strategy was to bring human beings to a point where they are never alone with their God, nor ever attentively face to face with another human being....The mobile phone, then, seems to me to represent a major breakthrough for the powers of hell–it is a new thing, which allows the devil to take a significant step forward in her [_sic_] grand design. With a mobile, a person is never alone and is never entirely attentive to someone else. What is entirely brilliant about it from a demonic perspective is that so many people have been persuaded that this is not something pleasurable (a free choice) but something necessary.

The devil's cleverness, in short, lies in persuading us (it didn't take very much) that what is profoundly destructive, anti-progressive, is a step forward. Forward to what? It seems to me at least possible that notions of progress might revolve around how we treat each other in social situations, for example, not around the latest electronic toy. And yet, even a slight awareness of a "non-demonic" (in Sara Maitland's formulation) type of progress is apparently beyond our ken. Some years ago I taught in the sociology department of a major American university, and marveled at my colleagues, who were constantly interrupting their conversations with each other to take cell phone calls–as if a conversation with someone who was not physically present were more important than one with someone who was. They had no idea of how rude they were being on a daily basis, and regarded my own views on technology as "quaint." Considering the damage this behavior was doing to human social interaction, and the fact that these folks were sociologists, I was impressed by the irony of it all. It was like being at a convention of nutritionists, each of whom weighed more than 300 pounds. After all, if obesity is the new health, what is there left to say?

This brings to mind the famous phrase coined by the late Senator Daniel Patrick Moynihan, "defining deviancy down." Moynihan pointed out that there was a process in American culture by which behavior traditionally regarded as selfish or vulgar—e.g., abruptly breaking off a conversation with one person to initiate one with someone else—rapidly becomes acceptable if enough people start doing it. Deviancy, in short, goes down to the lowest common denominator, finally becoming the norm. Indeed, the vulgarization and "narcissization" of American society had become so widespread by the mid-1990s that books were being written on incivility, and conferences being held on the subject as well. But none of this made any difference for actual behavior, as even the most casual observation of contemporary American society reveals.*

I remember, some years ago, then Secretary of State Condoleezza Rice talking about American (non)relations with Cuba, and stating that "we don't want that model to be able to replicate itself"—the old contagion theory of communism, as it were. Well, I'm not big on dictatorships myself, but what about the danger of the *American* model replicating itself? When you go to New Zealand and see the Maori people talking on cell phones and watching American sitcoms, you know that Moynihan's prediction about the world turning into trash is not very far off.

China, which is all set to replace the United States as the next hegemonic power, is of course replicating the American model with a vengeance. "To get rich is glorious," declared Deng Xiaoping, and the 1990s witnessed the stripping away of time-worn (non-Maoist) Chinese models of good citizenship and moral participation in collective goals. The race was on to crank out as many cell phones, DVD players, televisions, shopping malls, and highways as possible. Monthly car production went from 20,000 in 1993 to 250,000 in 2004, and Wal-Mart and McDonald's have spread through the country like wildfire. In *China Pop*, Jianying Zha gives us a vivid (read: garish and appalling) portrait of a country wallowing in mass consumerism, from soap operas to pornography and beyond. China is now dotted with privileged consumption zones, theme parks, and beauty pageants. Cosmetic surgery clinics abound, promising to give young women more rounded, Western eyes. In fact, the beauty industry grosses more than $24 billion a year. "Consumerism became a religion," writes Rachel Dewoskin in *Foreign Babes in Beijing*, as "street kiosks made way for sleek boutiques and cafés, where Chinese and foreigners lounged together, drinking lattes and Italian sodas." Companies arrived like missionaries, she recalls, seducing the average Chinese with products they never knew they needed. In the progressive China of today, everyone, according to the British anthropologist David Harvey, "speculates on the desires of others in the Darwinian struggle for position."

This is why we have more to fear from the American model of progress, and its replication on a world scale, than from some aged *caudillo* in Cuba. For what does it consist of, finally, when "freedom" means little more than "free enterprise"? As Harvey tells us in his careful and erudite study, *A Brief History of Neoliberalism*,

> that culture, however spectacular, glamorous, and beguiling, perpetually plays with desires without ever conferring satisfactions beyond the limited identity of the shopping mall and the anxieties of status by way of good looks (in the case of women) or of material possessions. 'I shop therefore I am' and possessive individualism together construct a world of pseudo-satisfactions that is superficially exciting but hollow at its core.

This beguiling quality–the notion of culture as chic– is an enormous shell game, as Harvey demonstrates in his summary of what happened to New York City during the 1970s. A fiscal crisis arose, the product of rapid suburban- ization that was destroying the tax base of the city. Finan- cial institutions were prepared to bridge the gap between income and expenditure in the city budget, and expansion of public employment via federal funding was also being considered. But in 1975 a powerful group of investment bankers, led by Citibank, refused to roll over the debt and left the city technically bankrupt. Union activity was curtailed; cutbacks took place in education, public health, and transportation; and wealth got redistributed upward, to the rich and super rich. It was, says Harvey, "a coup by the financial institutions against the democratically elected government of New York City." Both the social and the physical infrastructure of the city deteriorated, and the city government, the municipal labor movement, and working-class New Yorkers were stripped of their power.

That wasn't the end of it, however. The next step on the part of the business community was to turn New York into a "good investment opportunity." "Corporate welfare," writes Harvey, "substituted for people welfare." The idea was to sell New York as a tourist destination, and "I [Heart] New York" swept through the town as the new logo. As Harvey notes:

> The narcissistic exploration of self, sexuality, and identity became the leitmotif of bourgeois urban culture. Artistic freedom and artistic licence, promoted by the city's powerful cultural institutions, led, in effect, to the neoliberalization of culture. 'Delirious New York'...erased the collective memory of democratic New York....New York became the epicentre of postmodern cultural and intellectual experimentation. Meanwhile the investment bankers reconstructed the city economy around financial activities...and diversified consumerism (gentrification and neighbourhood 'restoration' playing a prominent and profitable role). City government was more and more construed as an entrepreneurial rather than a social democratic or even managerial entity.

Progress (so-called) has to be chic, in other words, and this meshes well with the neoliberal equation of freedom with lifestyle choice; which effectively kills democracy, or renders it irrelevant. Again, it's a question of how you define it. Home visits by doctors, for example (the norm, when I was a child), have vanished almost completely, and Americans would hardly regard the return of this practice as progress. It may well be a life saver, but it's not particularly hip. SUV's that destroy the environment are chic; mass transit is not. Dog-eat-dog competition is chic; a social safety net, or a health system that actually works, is not. Best sellers praising globalization are chic; community and friendship, rather passé. And so on. Children get excited by toys, bright colors, and the latest gimmick; adults, by the prospect of a truly healthy society. As deviancy is defined downward across the planet, whether in New York or Beijing, it leaves very few adults in its wake.

As far as technology goes, the irony is that it seems to be failing in its own terms. The social and psychological damage of "life on the screen" has by now been documented by numerous studies; but when the technology is actually delivering the opposite of what was originally promised, one has to ask what it is all for. The literature on this is fairly large, so all I can do at this point is touch on some of the highlights.**

In _Tyranny of the Moment_, Norwegian anthropologist Thomas Hylland Eriksen argues that while the period from 1980 saw a rapid expansion in so-called time-saving technologies, the truth is that we have never had so little free time as we do now. The Internet has made possible a huge expansion of available information, and yet all the data show an increasingly ignorant population. Changes that were touted as boosting creativity and efficiency have actually had the opposite effect. Air travel is now so heavily congested that by 2000, fifty percent of the flights connecting major European cities were delayed. In the United States, road traffic tripled during 1970-2000, and the average speed involved in getting around decreased every year. In fact, the average speed of a car in New York City in 2000 was about seven miles per hour, and we can guess that it is even less today. Etc.

One activity heavily promoted as "progressive" is multitasking, made easy by the use of a variety of compact technologies. Yet a study conducted by the University of London in 2005, according to the journalist Christine Rosen, revealed that workers who are distracted by e-mail and cell phone calls suffer a fall in I.Q. of more than twice that experienced by pot smokers. In 2007, she notes, a major U.S. business analyst (Jonathan Spira, at a research firm called Basex) estimated that multitasking was costing the American economy $650 billion a year in lost productivity, and a University of Michigan study revealed that it causes short-term memory loss. In general, writes Walter Kirn, "Neuroscience is confirming what we all suspect: Multitasking is dumbing us down and driving us crazy." Specifically, it interferes with areas of the brain related to memory and learning; it actually slows our thinking. The problem seems to be that when you move from one task to another, you have to keep "revving up" to get back to doing what you were doing before. Hence, the quality of work gets compromised due to loss of focus and loss of time. In general, the Net lowers the brain's capacity for concentration and contemplation; "reading on the Net" is almost a contradiction in terms. "We inevitably begin to take on the quality of those technologies," writes Nicholas Carr; "our own intelligence...flattens into artificial intelligence."

All in all, it now appears that endless technological innovation and economic expansion, which have only themselves as their goal, finally undermine social relations, redefine common sense, and interfere with our ability to think. Harvey hits the nail on the head when he argues for the existence of an inner connection between "technological dynamism, instability, dissolution of social solidarities, environmental degradation, deindustrialization, rapid shifts in time-space relations, speculative bubbles, and the general tendency towards crisis formation within capitalism." We are caught in a contradiction, he says, between "a seductive but alienating possessive individualism on the one hand and the desire for a meaningful collective life on the other."

Personally, I don't think there is much doubt as to which of these two options is going to win out. By 2050, the planet is expected to have a population of 10 to 11 billion people. Competition for food and water will be fierce; resources in general will be scarce. The majority of this population will probably be living on less than two dollars a day, and "iron" governments will arise to manage politically unstable situations . And yet, there may be an odd silver lining to this, as *Blade Runner* descends on us in earnest: clutched in the hand of every man, woman, and child will be a state-of-the-art cell phone, and in front of each individual the hippest of personal computers. Granted, we may be collectively dying, but at least we'll be chic.

*See footnote reference to Olds and Schwartz cited in Essay #4.

**To mention a few key sources: Thomas Hylland Eriksen, *Tyranny of the Moment* (London: Pluto Press, 2001); Nicole Aubert, *Le culte de l'urgence* (Paris: Flammarion, 2003); Christine Rosen, "The Myth of Multitasking," *The New Atlantis,* No. 20 (Spring 2008), pp. 105-10; Walter Kirn, "The Autumn of the Multitaskers," *The Atlantic Monthly*, November 2007; Nicholas Carr, "Is Google Making Us Stupid?" *The Atlantic Monthly*, July/August 2008, and his book *The Shallows* (New York: W.W. Norton, 2010).

22. A Month in Xela

After having lived in Mexico for nearly three years, and still speaking bad Spanish, I decided it was time to do something about this sorry state of affairs. The problem, I realized, was that it was difficult for me to get an "immersion experience" in Mexico: I simply had too many bilingual friends here. I would have to go to a place where there was no escaping the Spanish language, twenty-four hours a day; a place like Guatemala.

I had been to Guatemala two years before, mainly following the tourist route: Antigua, Lago Atitlán, and the villages that surround the lake. Antigua was soaking in language schools, I remembered; but when I consulted the guidebooks on the subject, they all said the same thing: you won't learn Spanish in Antigua. The place is crawling with gringos; you'll just wind up socializing with them and speaking your native tongue. Quetzaltenango—or Xela, as it is popularly known—is where you want to go. Americans don't know about it; it's off the beaten track. So, encouraged by this "tip", I got on the Internet and enrolled in a language school in Xela for four weeks. I flew into Guatemala City two weeks later, and arrived in Xela the next day. (As it turned out, everybody else had apparently read the same guidebooks and had taken the same advice. There were more Americans in Xela than in all of Houston; or so it seemed.)

I don't know what I had expected of the physical environment—something like Antigua, perhaps—but

Xela was not it. It soon became clear to me that Antigua was a "showcase" city, the exception rather than the rule. With a population of 200,000, Xela claims to be the second-largest city in Guatemala; yet its infrastructure is completely shot. The streets are riddled with cracks and potholes; sidewalks, when they exist, are typically broken. More often than not, you are walking on dirt or trekking through mud. Riding the buses is not to be undertaken on a full stomach, as they are old and decrepit, and jerk you up and down as though you were in a milkshake machine. The cause of all this is not hard to ascertain: Guatemala is, in effect, ruled by an oligarchy, and a large fraction of the national budget is earmarked for the military (which the country needs like a hole in the head). There is very little left over for roads, bridges, transportation, education, and public health. Truth be told, Guatemala is a lot like the United States, only a bit more strung out.

Of course, the United States has no excuse, whereas after thirty-six years of civil war (1960-96) Guatemala had the stuffing kicked out of it. Nearly half the population is illiterate, and half the country's children suffer from malnutrition. With heavy American support, the Guatemalan military undertook a scorched-earth campaign, complete with U.S.-trained torture and death squads, that destroyed any possibility of social justice. The result? After 626 massacres there were something like 150,000 dead, 100,000 *desaparecidos*, 1 million persons who had gone into hiding, and 1 million refugees (most of them fleeing to Mexico and the United States). More than 440 indígena pueblos were wiped out, 200,000 children were orphaned, and 40,000 women became widows. The urban population is understandably demoralized and cynical, living in a strange kind of spiritual vacuum. What Gertrude Stein once remarked about Oakland, California, applies to Xela a hundred times over: There is no "there" there.

The odd thing is that this huge void at the center has been filled by a purely consumer culture, one very much based on the U.S. model of the good life. In fact, Xela comes across as a bad version of a bad American city—Sacramento, Dallas, Little Rock, Indianapolis, etc. "Culture" consists of cell phones and Internet cafés, which are always crowded; there doesn't seem to be much else. Whatever happened to the Maya?, I thought to myself. To an outsider, the whole thing made for a strange sight: elderly indígena women on broken-down buses clutching cell phones, and nine-year-old Mayan girls tottering around on high-heeled shoes. And as in the majority of U.S. cities, the people are basically unfriendly. The staff in stores consists mostly of adolescents, who won't make eye contact and can barely grunt out "para servirle". It is as though what the United States was not able to destroy by means of "hard power", it was now finishing off by means of "soft power"—electronic toys, blockbuster films, Cocacola, and neoliberal economics.*

These impressions were largely confirmed by conversations I had with people born and raised in the town. One woman, a social worker in her early forties, agreed with me about American electronic gadgetry being the focus of Xela culture. "It's quite amazing," she told me; "I work with families who go to bed hungry, who literally go without food, so that they can buy and maintain a cell phone. It enables them to say, 'yo soy alguien' (I am somebody), because in truth, they have no other identity or source of self-esteem. It's pretty pathetic, but that's what Guatemala has come to." (I subsequently learned that Guatemala is No. 1 in Central America in cell phone consumption, and No. 3 in all of Latin America.)

"When did all this start?", I asked her, "and how?"

"I think in the sixties," she replied, "around the time that I was born. The greatest single influence was American television. Those images of the wealthy consumer life had a big impact on the Guatemalan population. Most of us still believe the images are real."

"But what did Guatemalan culture consist of before the CIA overthrew the Arbenz government in 1954, and before the invasion of American TV?," I continued.

She shrugged her shoulders. "I honestly don't know. What you see in Xela today—McDonald's, Wendy's, shopping malls and all the rest—is all I've ever known. It's who we are now. I don't know who we were before that."

I confess, I found this really chilling. It reminded me of that town in *One Hundred Years of Solitude* that lost its identity because the inhabitants forgot the names of things.

The language instruction I received in Xela, in any case, was first-rate: one-on-one classes, four to five hours per day, until I felt my head was going to explode. That aspect of my time in Xela was very positive, and in fact I became good friends with the director of the school, who was also a professor of economics at the local university. All of this made the trip very worthwhile. But I couldn't—can't—shake the image of a city without purpose, without meaning, and of a country which, having been largely destroyed by U.S. politics, now seeks to emulate the American economy and American culture, both of which are dying. If the sources of vitality can no longer be found in traditional Mayan culture, then it's not clear where they can be found, or what the future holds for a nation that became a pawn in the Cold War through no fault of its own and was subsequently hung out to dry.

My four weeks in Xela having come to an end, I decided to clear my head by spending a couple of days in Antigua before returning to Mexico. Yes, I thought, it's a tourist trap and a showcase town, but two days of sitting in the central square drinking that exquisite Guatemalan coffee and reading newspapers may be good for the soul. Which proved to be the case. And then, during one of those days, I ran across something that caught me completely off guard: a gallery crammed with Guatemalan art, art that was absolutely dazzling. Oils, acrylics, ceramics, you name it—the colors were truly vibrant.

"Where is all this from?", I asked the curator. "Who did all this?"

"It's all Guatemalan," he told me, "artists from 25 to 80 years of age. From all over the country," he added. A few of them, it turned out, actually lived in Xela.

I stood there and gaped. After four weeks of living in a spiritless environment, I was now confronted by this marvelous concentration of spirit, of art as fine as I had seen in galleries in Mexico City or New York. "Your country wasn't able to destroy us completely," the paintings seemed to be saying. "Not with guns, and not with gadgets. There are still a few of us who know what life is about."

Of course, I wound up buying a small painting and hanging it on the wall of my study back home, along with some photos I took of the Guatemalan countryside. I look at it every day. And if I listen closely, I can still hear it whispering, from time to time, telling me about a life that refuses to be extinguished. It reminds me of a graffito I once saw on a wall in Chiapas, addressed to the ruling class: "Nuestros sueños no caben en sus urnas"–Our dreams do not fit into your ballot boxes. Would that that were true of all of Latin America.

*What I am describing here, however, may not apply to rural Mayan culture, and there is some literature pointing to native resistance to Americanization and consumerism. Anthropologist Robert Hinshaw, who lives in the Mayan village of Tzununá, says that his neighbors are proud of their traditional culture and not interested in having it altered in any significant way—although they all seem to own cell phones(!). Edward Fischer, who lived in Patzún and Tecpán for twenty-eight months during the 1990s, claims that globalization has galvanized a resurgence of Mayan identity politics. His work, however, has been questioned by other anthropologists. The jury, in short, is still out on this matter. See Jack Houston, "Robert Hinshaw," *Revue* (Guatemala City), Vol. 18 No. 6 (August 2009), pp. 18-19 and 106; Edward F. Fischer, *Cultural Logics and Global Economics* (Austin: University of Texas Press, 2001); and the review of the latter by Charles R. Hale in the *Journal of Anthropological Research,* Vol. 59 No. 2 (Summer 2003), pp. 296-98.

References

There is a very large literature on the civil war in Guatemala, and the destruction of the population during that time. Data cited above can be found in the following sources:

Archdiocese of Guatemala, *Guatemala: Never Again!* (Maryknoll, NY: Orbis Books, 1999).

Francisco Goldman, *The Art of Political Murder* (New York: Grove Press, 2008).

Linda Haugaard, "Admissions and omissions–the CIA in Guatemala," *In These Times*, 22 July 1996.

Jennifer Schirmer, *The Guatemalan Military Project* (Philadelphia: University of Pennsylvania Press, 1999).

Third World Traveler, "A 'killing field' in the Americas: US policy in Guatemala,"
http://www.thirdworldtraveler.com/US_ThirdWorld/US_Guat.html.

Virtual Truth Commission, "Reports by Country: Guatemala,"

http://www.geocities.com/-virtualtruth/guatemal.htm.

23. The Hula Hoop Theory of History

Above all, no zeal.
-Talleyrand

There is a curious rhythm to human affairs, or perhaps more specifically, to Western history. Some movement or idea comes along, and everyone gets swept up in its wake. This is it, then; this is the Answer we've been looking for. All of those previous answers were wrong; now, at long last, we're on the right track. In the fullness of time, of course, this shiny new idea loses its luster, betrays us, or even results in the death of millions. So apparently, we were deceived. But wait: here's the *true* new idea, the one we should have followed all along. *This* is the Answer we've been looking for. Etc.

The American writer, Eric Hoffer, described this syndrome roughly sixty years ago in a book that also generated a lot of zeal (for a short time, anyway), *The True Believer.* People convert quite easily, observed Hoffer; they switch from one ism to another, from Catholicism to Marxism to whatever is next on the horizon. The belief system runs its course, then another one takes its place. What is significant is the energy involved, not the particular target, which could be anything, really. For what drives this engine is the need for psychological reassurance, for Meaning with a capital M—a comprehensive system of belief that explains everything. There is a feeling, largely unacknowledged, that without this we are lost; that life would have no purpose, and history no meaning; that both (as Shakespeare put it) would amount to little more than a tale told by an idiot, full of sound and fury, signifying nothing.

I call this the Hula Hoop Theory of History, but one could also label it the Pet Rock Theory, or any other craze that grabs our attention for a week or a century. It has a lot in common with the skeptical thinking of the sixteenth-century philosopher Montaigne, who had a great influence on Eric Hoffer, among others. In his *Essays*, Montaigne pointed out that the new sciences of Copernicus and Paracelsus claimed that the ancient sciences of Aristotle and Ptolemy were false. But how long, he argued, before some future scientist comes along, and says the same thing about Copernicus and Paracelsus? Do we ever really know the truth once and for all?

One might also call this the Drunken Sailor Theory of History, I suppose. Reflecting on the first flush of the French Revolution, William Wordsworth wrote: "Bliss it was in that dawn to be alive." After Robespierre, the Terror, and the rivers of blood that flowed through the streets of Paris, however, a sober Talleyrand could only comment that what the human race needed, above anything else, was to stay clear of zeal. The path from bliss to barbarism may not be linear, but it does seem to be fairly common, historically speaking.

The latest treatise in the Montaigne-Hoffer school of history is that of the British scholar John Gray, *Black Mass*. Gray draws liberally on the work of the American historian Carl Becker, whose *Heavenly City of the Eigh-teenth-Century Philosophers* (1932) has never been surpassed as an analysis of modernity. Becker claimed that the notion of redemption that lay at the heart of Christianity was recast by the philosophers of the French Enlightenment in terms of progress, or secular salvation. Enlightenment utopianism, in a word, was the transformation of Christian eschatology into the belief in the perfectibility of man—heaven on earth, as it were. This would be the Second Coming, the defeat of ignorance and evil (= sin) by means of reliable knowledge, science and technology in particular.

In Gray's view, the modern "secular fundamentalisms"—Jacobinism, Bolshevism, Fascism, and most recently, globalization—followed directly from this transformation. The result has been satanic—a black or inverted mass (i.e., one recited backwards)—in that these pseudo-religions have all caused a world of harm. The one idea common to all of them is that progress and perfectibility are within our grasp, and can be attained through an historical process whereby true knowledge will defeat ignorance (evil). Thus the world, and our psyches, are saved, no less in the modern secular world than they were claimed to be in the medieval Christian one, because history itself is imbued with Meaning.

Sad to say, the first three of these secular religions proved, in the fullness of time, not to be the Answer but rather the God that failed; and globalization (Thomas Friedman and his devotees notwithstanding) is in the process of going the same route, revealing itself to be a "false dawn." Of course, says Gray, once globalization and neoliberalism are finally exposed for what they are, and take their proper place on the scrap heap of history, it will hardly be the case that we shall abandon notions of progress, utopia, and Meaning in history. Not a chance. We in the West will have to find another hula hoop, another pet rock, because as a Christian civilization we are simply unable to live without the myth of redemption. Hence, he concludes, the "cycle of order and anarchy will never end." The tragedy is that we "prefer the romance of a meaningless quest to coping with difficulties that can never be finally overcome." Hence, "the violence of faith looks set to shape the coming century."

At the present time, it's not clear what the next hula hoop will be; but I'm not sure it matters all that much. If the Montaigne-Hoffer-Gray school of historical analysis is correct, what is certain is that there will be no derailing the zeal in advance, no stopping the next ideological-religious binge at the second martini, so to speak. The word "some" has very little meaning in the world of secular fundamentalism; for us, it's all or nothing. "Man cannot make a worm," wrote Montaigne, "yet he will make gods by the dozen."

For it is all a kind of shamanism, in a way, an attempt to become whole through magic. We are all broken, after all; that is why the promise of redemption has such a powerful hold on us. "I am he who puts together," declared one Mazatec shaman, some years ago. It finally comes down to a (misguided) attempt at healing, which is reinforced by tribal practice (commonly known as groupthink). I recall attending a conference on postmodernism in the 1990s and being struck by how similar the lectures were, in form, to those of Communist Party members of the 1930s. The "holy names" were different—one cited de Man and Derrida instead of Marx and Lenin—but the glazed eyes and the mantra-like repetition of politically approved phrases were very much the same. Truth be told, I have observed the same hypnotic behavior at all types of academic conferences, from feminism to computer science. You watch, you listen, and you wonder: When will we finally wake up? And you know the horrible truth: never. In effect, we shall continue to erect statues to Napoleon, but never, or rarely, to Montaigne. This much is clear.

Which brings me to what I consider the bottom line, namely the structure of the brain. The frontal lobes, the large neocortex that governs rational thinking and logical processes, is a relative latecomer on the scene, in evolutionary terms. The limbic system, which is the center of impulse and emotion, has been around much longer. The conflict between the two is perhaps best illustrated by the case of the alcoholic sitting at a bar, staring at a frosty stein of beer in front of him. The neocortex says No; the limbic system says Go. Statistically, most drunks die of alcohol poisoning or cirrhosis of the liver; very few escape from the siren song of the limbic brain. As Goethe once put it, "the world is not logical; it is psycho-logical." And that is to put it quite mildly, it seems to me.

We will not escape the ravages of climate change; we shall not avoid the economic and ecological disasters that are integral to global capitalism; not be able to avert an oil crisis, an energy crisis, or a food and water crisis that will become extreme when the world population finally arrives at 10 or 11 billion, by mid-century. These things are not going to be resolved by reason, by the neocortex, no matter how many articles are published on these subjects in learned journals or popular magazines. And they certainly can't be resolved by the limbic brain, whose function is indulgence, not restraint. Hence, it is a fair guess that we shall start doing things differently only when there is no other choice; and even then, we shall undoubtedly cast our efforts in the form of a shiny new and improved hula hoop, the belief system that will finally be the true one, after all of those false starts; the one we should have been following all along. What to call it? Catastrophism, perhaps. You can consider this the founding document.

PART IV
QUO VADIS?

24. The Asian Road to Victory

There is by now a growing consensus that as the sun is setting in the West, it is simultaneously rising in the East. When Mao Zedong called the United States a "paper tiger" back in the 1950s, everybody laughed. Fifty years later, the remark doesn't seem so funny.

Consider: by 2005, the trade imbalance between China and the United States was 202 billion dollars, having multiplied nearly twenty-fold in just fifteen years. China now holds 922 billion dollars' worth of U.S. Treasury bills, and a total of almost two trillion in U.S. dollars. Its economy expands nearly 10% a year, while the American economy has basically crashed, and will need Chinese loans to bail it out. And while the American manufacturing sector gets weaker with each passing day, China has become the workshop of the world. It won't be long before it starts to flex its muscles militarily as well.

Such are the conclusions of a number of distinguished economists and political scientists. What few of them provide, however, is an *explanation* for this turn of events. A notable exception is the book I referred to in the third essay in this collection, *In the Jaws of the Dragon*, by Eamonn Fingleton. Fingleton makes the point that while the Americans spend like there is no tomorrow, the top-down bureaucratic system of China forces its citizens to save rather than consume. In this authoritarian, state-capitalist arrangement, a number of policies make consumer spending very difficult, with the resulting savings generating huge cash reserves that are then deployed in boosting key industries. It's a coercive system, says Fingleton, and it works. (In fact, Franklin Delano Roosevelt did something similar during World War II, and the U.S. savings rate went from 5% to 25% in three years. The resulting capital was used to pay for armaments manufacture.)

Yet as Fingleton recognizes, the policy of restricted consumption and enforced savings has a deeper root to it, what he refers to as the "Confucian truth ethic." Although there are real differences among the various schools of Eastern philosophy, they do have a number of important things in common; and as with the Judeo-Christian ethic of the West, these things go very deep. Whether we are talking about the *I Ching*, the *Tao Te Ching*, the *Analects*, or the *Chuang Tzu*, two items in particular stand out as central to this way of thinking: the notion that the truth is relative, or provisional; and that harmony is the ultimate purpose of society. Before I say any more about contemporary China, it might be worth our while to explore these themes in a bit more detail.

In a sense, harmony and radical relativism form the shadow side of the Western tradition, which prizes individualism and the reliability of (binary) logic and empirical evidence. This lends Eastern thought a "forbidden fruit" aspect, an exotic aura that exerted a strong influence on many young people in the United States during the sixties and seventies, especially. I remember my own introduction to it during that time, and the sense that a great weight had been lifted from my shoulders. For Western individualism and scientific reasoning can finally seem oppressive, too tight a box to live in; in which case thought systems such as Taoism and Buddhism appear to be a breath of fresh air. "Go with the flow," we all told each other during those heady days in California.

A particularly significant milestone of the genre during that time was the publication, in 1974, of Robert Pirsig's *Zen and the Art of Motorcycle Maintenance*. It was Pirsig's claim that this Eastern shadow tradition showed up in ancient Greece as Sophism, the *bête noire* of Plato and his school. In fact, so forbidden was this fruit for Pirsig that he finally went insane in the pursuit of the "lost" tradition. Whether or not the Sophists really were Taoists, however, is not the point. What matters historically is that they represented an alternate fork in the road to Platonic doctrine, and one which Plato did his best to squash. The founder of the school, Protagoras (after whom Plato named one of his dialogues), was fond of saying that "man is the measure of all things"; by which he meant that every person has his or her own truth, and that all of these are equally valid. Rhetoric was the issue, he taught his disciples, not logic; persuasion, not reason, was what counted in any given argument. For Plato, this was the philosophy of the mob, of people who were morally and intellectually dead and interested only in acquiring the gift of gab. As Pirsig notes, Plato won the battle—at least in theory—and the Western notion of truth (postmodernism and perhaps law courts excepted) is that it really does exist, and is not merely a function of who is speaking or how persuasive an orator he or she is. As the British philosopher A.N. Whitehead famously remarked, Western philosophy is essentially "a series of footnotes to Plato."

But the East went in a different direction, and for those accustomed to only one way of thinking, it definitely casts a spell. "Choosing is a disease of the mind," as one Eastern text puts it. All is in flux; there is no Yes or No. We must avoid getting attached to Right or Wrong, because they fluctuate depending on the person and the circumstances. "For each individual there is a different 'true' and a different 'false'," says the *Chuang Tzu*. By following the Tao, going with the flow, one attains the best possible outcome. As the former Chinese leader Deng Xiaoping once put it, the Chinese are "crossing the river by feeling for the stones" (*mozhe shitou guo he*).

That the truth is contextual, says Fingleton, means that expediency, or the optimization of what is regarded as beneficial, is the true priority. Thus Zhou Enlai, the consummate Chinese politician, was said to have never told the truth–or a lie. In effect, he made no distinction between the two; he just "felt for the stones."

Again, on an individual level, Eastern philosophy can afford a large measure of relief. The Western reality system exalts notions of intentionality and deliberate action; it holds that the world can and should be bent to the human will. But this doesn't really work in human life, does it? We all eventually have to confront the fact that there are many things in life–perhaps the most important ones–that are simply beyond our control. "Those who would take hold of the world and act on it," wrote Lao Tzu, "never, I notice, succeed." Hence the Chinese concept of *wu wei*, or not-doing; which, properly understood, is not the same thing as passivity. Rather, it refers to surrender, to letting things take their course, follow the Tao.

The word "Tao" appears for the first time in the *Analects* of Confucius, and means the right way of conduct for both the individual and society. According to the American sinologist Herlee Creel, contemplative Taoism, which operates on the individual level, strives for inner harmony. But there is also, he says, a purposive Taoism, which seeks to use the techniques of nonaction and nonjudgmentalism as a means to power. In other words, be without desire in order to get what you desire. This theme–which is essentially one of pure manipulation–features big in the *Tao Te Ching*, a book that (like *The Prince*, by Machiavelli) gives advice to kings and lords, and sees the Tao as a technique of control. "The sage, in governing," says the *Tao Te Ching*, "empties the people's minds and fills their bellies, weakens their wills and strengthens their bones." We are starting to approach the political philosophy of the Chinese state, in which 97% of the population (a total of 1.3 billion people) have full bellies (no mean achievement, by the way).

This, then, is a system of "soft authoritarianism," in which relationships take precedence over laws–which are, as Fingleton points out, only selectively enforced anyway. Confucianism, he says, is "every enlightened despot's perfect ideology." Its emphasis on harmony is easily twisted into an insistence on conformity. ("The nail that stands out is likely to get hammered down," as the Japanese like to say.) It enjoins the people to passivity, and legitimizes authoritarian leadership. Indeed, it is hard to dissent from a system in which there is no right or wrong, true or false, but only that which supposedly promotes the commonweal. Those who try—like the Falun Gong movement that was founded in 1992, and whose doctrines are basically Buddhist—become the target of government crackdown in short order. The Communist Party's monopoly of power is presented to the Chinese people as a "natural" fact of life: the way, the Tao.

Much of Fingleton's concern in his book is over the way in which he sees America becoming "Confucianized," the way U.S. corporations play ball with the Chinese state so as to acquire influence and get on the gravy train. Thus Yahoo!, Google, and Microsoft all agreed (for a while, anyway) to abide by China's censorship rules in serving Chinese Internet users—for example, to expunge all references to Tiananmen Square and Taiwanese independence. In addition, top technology firms in the United States contracted with China to develop fire walls that block access of Chinese citizens to "dangerous" information, including important Western websites. Under the influence of the China lobby, pro-Chinese journalists and academics in the United States get their reputations enhanced, go to exclusive dinner parties, and receive lavish fees for lectures. Those who are critical are quickly left out of the loop, and barred from sources of research and information. In general, the Chinese system is one of institutionalized bribery, in which corruption functions like legitimate payment for services rendered. The process, says Fingleton, is destroying American values. It is China that is changing us, he concludes, not we who are changing China. We are not democratizing them—far from it. Rather, they are Confucianizing us.

All this is probably true, but it seems to be part of a larger, graver loss, that of the Enlightenment tradition itself. Eastern philosophy may be the shadow side of that tradition, but it should be clear by now that the shadow has a shadow. How can the West confront a nation whose government is endlessly slippery, and that meets confrontation with Sophism, in effect? And if, as Mao Zedong predicted, "the East wind will prevail over the West," what will it be like to live in a world dominated by an ethos in which the truth doesn't, for all practical purposes, exist, and in which everyone is expected to fall in step with some enforced "harmony"? There is a word for this type of regime: Orwellian. The loss of the Enlightenment yardstick of truth to some kind of pervasive amorality would represent a loss far deeper than an economic one, it seems to me. A Confucianized society in which truth is nothing more than expediency is its own kind of prison; "go with the flow" can become its own form of ego, and of repression.

Some time ago, I was talking with a Mexican colleague of mine, a very brilliant teacher and administrator who had read up on China and was aware of some of these issues. "There may come a time," he said with a sigh, "when we shall actually miss the gringos." It's a sobering thought.

25. Tribal Consciousness and Enlightenment Tradition

At one point in his work, Proust advances a theory of development that goes back to Goethe, and ultimately to Plato. It was Goethe who coined the term "morphology," by which he meant the science of form, and the crucial idea was that the adult manifestation of an organism was already encoded in its earliest structural arrangement. Thus the entire oak tree, for example, was already present in the acorn; growth and development were basically a process of "unfolding" from an original archetype. It is a teleological theory, a theory of predestination; and Proust comments that if you see a pretty girl next to her mother, you can already discern in the daughter the pattern of ageing, the adult features, "in the wings," as it were. Extending the theory from the biological to the social realm, Proust argues that we should hardly be surprised, for example, to learn that some Jewish person we might know (this around 1900, say) is heatedly on the side of Alfred Dreyfus.* For this is pre-ordained, he says; it's in the blood. Our mistake is to believe that we are making rational decisions, when the truth is that "our minds possess in advance...the characteristic that we imagine ourselves to be selecting." He goes on:

> For we grasp only the secondary ideas, without detecting the primary cause (Jewish blood, French birth or whatever it may be) that inevitably produced them....We take from our family, as [adult plants] take the form of their seed, as well the ideas

by which we live as the malady from which we shall die.

The theory, then, is one of genetic memory, and for Proust it applies to the biological development of human beings as well as plants. It also, Proust is saying, applies to the mental and supposedly intellectual function of human beings, in the form of what we might call "tribal consciousness." Of course, Dreyfus was innocent and his enemies were a bunch of liars and antisemites, but for Proust that is not the point. The claim here is that we would *expect* Jews to be on the side of Dreyfus without worrying too much about the evidence pro or con, in the same way that it is not too much of a shock to learn that 96% of the black American population voted for Barack Obama. These are not really freely chosen rational decisions, in short, and we are kidding ourselves if we think they are.

This matter of tribal consciousness is enormously significant, it seems to me, and Jewish identity is as good an illustration of it as any. Suppose, at the height of the Dreyfus Affair, God had waved a magic wand and all of the Jews in France suddenly became Christian, and all the Christians, Jews. I can't prove it, of course, but I'm guessing that a large percentage of the new Christians would suddenly regard Dreyfus as guilty, and a large percentage of the new Jews would now find him innocent. It is depressing to think that evidence gets marshaled in the service of emotions, but hard to avoid that conclusion. What happened in the aftermath of the Israeli attack on Gaza during December 2008-January 2009, for example, which was nothing less than the wholesale massacre of Palestinian civilians, was quite Orwellian: one heard Israeli spokesmen and apologists claiming that Israel (the occupying power) was somehow the victim in all of this—and they actually believed it! But again, if a magic wand suddenly rendered the Israelis Palestinians and vice versa, wouldn't the former Israelis now be on the Palestinian side, and the former Palestinians now be convinced that yes, Israel was indeed the victim in this tragedy? That blood, rather than evidence, is the issue constitutes the essence of tribal consciousness. We need to examine this more closely.

I remember, some years ago, pondering this question of how tribal allegiance colonizes the brain when I ran across an intriguing work of science fiction by Neal Stephenson, entitled *Snow Crash*. The core of the book is what might be called the "viral theory of religion," in which the brain is taken over or possessed by a certain set of religious ideas. The virus replicates itself inside the individual mind, and it also jumps from one person to the next. Stephenson spends a lot of time applying this theory of infection to ancient Sumer, the thought process of which can be regarded as a kind of trance phenomenon. (Egypt would fall into the same category, it seems to me.) There were, he says, various attempts to break out of the trance, Judaism being the most notable. Thus the Torah was also a virus, says Stephenson, but a benign one; a counter-virus to the ancient mythological world, which was stuck in a rut. Scribes copied it; people came to the synagogue to read it. Judaism was basically the first rational religion, then, but eventually it hardened into legalism, whereupon it was challenged by Christ...whose ideas got taken over by viral influence almost immediately, becoming a new theocracy. The Reformation, fifteen centuries later, was then the counter-virus to this. Etc. The idea is that we become "hosts" for self-replicating information, and as further examples Stephenson points to mass hysteria, jokes, catchy tunes, and ideologies.

As it turns out, _Snow Crash_ is the fictionalized version of the theory of memes, first put forward by the British biologist Richard Dawkins in 1976. The dictionary defines "meme" as "an idea, behavior, style, or usage that spreads from person to person within a culture." It's basically an information virus. Dawkins regarded it as a "unit" of cultural ideas that moves by way of imitation, and saw things such as catch phrases, fashion in clothing, and the technology of building arches (to take three unrelated examples) as falling into this category. Memes are essentially replicators, and their mode of transmission can be likened to contagion. As in the case of Stephenson, the virus/meme invades the "host," takes it over; and this is not, said Dawkins, necessarily positive: in terms of replication, a successful meme can actually be detrimental to the host body. (Just think of what neoliberalism and the Milton Friedman-virus–the "shock doctrine," in Naomi Klein's memorable phrase–have done to North and South America, for example.)

Now quite frankly, there is a lot to be said against the theory, most notably that it sets up a kind of pseudoscience that ultimately doesn't explain very much. There was, for example, a period in the history of science in which the concept of "instinct" was extended from biology to sociology and psychology. It was a total explanation: there was a death instinct, a love instinct, an artistic instinct, a criminal instinct, a nesting instinct, an instinct for sailing the high seas, and on and on. It took a while for social scientists to realize that these "explanations" were completely circular. As one philosopher observed, it was like labeling a bird that went around in circles a "rotopedist," and then when asked why the bird went around in circles, "explaining" that it did so because it was a rotopedist! Obviously, if everything is an instinct, or a meme, then nothing is.

Second, the meme theory itself can be seen as a meme, moving through society like a virus. But this takes us into a classic situation known as "Mannheim's paradox," because then the scientific status of the theory is called into question (it too is a fad, in other words). Karl Mannheim, the German sociologist, developed a mode of investigation known as the Sociology of Knowledge, whereby one studies how ideas get accepted in an intellectual community. Foreshadowing T.S. Kuhn, Mannheim argued that this acceptance did not occur on a rational basis, but rather on an ideological one. However, we then have to ask if this applies to the Sociology of Knowledge as well. After all, why should it alone get a free pass? If it does apply (and Mannheim unsuccessfully tried to argue that it didn't), the rug is pulled out from under the theory. It begins to look like the ancient "Liar's paradox": A Cretan said, "All Cretans are liars." Was he telling the truth?

Finally, and related to this, is the phenomenon whereby the counter-virus becomes, in short order, the new virus. Judaism becomes Pharasaism, Christ becomes St. Paul becomes the Vatican, the Reformation becomes Protestant rigidity, and New Age spirituality becomes Oprah and Chopra. The old mimetic system gets cracked open, and then the opener becomes The Opener. This means that in effect, with the exception of the briefest of moments, there is no such thing as a non-meme world. As I argued in an earlier essay ("The Hula Hoop Theory of History"), we seem to be caught up in one form of "hula-hoop" or another; we never seem to get a handle on any kind of objective reality. But can that really be the case? I mean, we know that Galileo was right about falling bodies and Aristotle wrong; we know that severe population pressure leads to hierarchical social systems; we know that syphilis is caused by a particular bacterium and that if left untreated, will result in insanity and death; and we know that Alfred Dreyfus was innocent and that the French army was corrupt. Objectively speaking, we know things–a lot of things. And yet, there is no getting around the fact that tribalism–mimetic thinking–is the rule rather than the exception. Thus while there are a number of soldiers in the Israeli army who refuse to serve in the occupied territories, and Israeli peace organizations such as Yesh Gvul ("There is a limit!") who support them, the majority of the population does indeed see itself as victims, and votes for a prime minister who can be guaranteed to continue the dead-end policies of oppression and occupation–until the demographics of the situation will finally render Israeli rule untenable, and things will change not by reason, but by force. One tribe, in short, will defeat another. What a triumph!

What our discussion comes down to is this: Leaving aside, for now, the first two (philosophical) objections to the meme-virus theory, and granting the fact that tribal consciousness really is the norm for the human race, what are the chances that mimetic behavior could be seriously disrupted, once and for all? This was, after all, the goal of the Scientific Revolution and the Enlightenment tradition; but as one political scientist once pointed out, "It's not that the Enlightenment failed; rather, it's that *it has never been tried.*" This is, of course, not entirely true; but when you have an "advanced" industrial nation with 59% of its adult population sitting around and waiting for the "Rapture" and the Second Coming, 29% thinking that the sun revolves around the earth or not knowing which revolves around which, and 45% believing that extra-terrestrials have visited the planet during the past year, you realize that this commentator has a point.

It all comes down to reflexivity: Can we break the hold of the meme-trance, and look at things from the "outside"? After all, intuitively speaking, heavy bodies should hit the earth faster than light ones when dropped from the same height, and we can plainly see the sun "rise" in the East and "set" in the West. Getting outside of the (medieval) meme here means that we look at evidence that is counter-intuitive; that we recognize that there is an objective truth to the situation that doesn't give a damn about our personal or tribal belief system; that one can stand outside a situation and evaluate it, and extend this analytical mode to our own beliefs, and to who we are. "O would some power the gift to give us/To see ourselves as others see us," wrote the Scottish poet Robert Burns in the eighteenth century. This external evaluation–what I have referred to elsewhere as "nonparticipating consciousness"–was, as Neal Stephenson correctly notes, the stellar contribution of the ancient Hebrews; and it was also characteristic of the ancient Greeks (their ties to the Mystery religions notwithstanding). After all, when you have Heraclitus talking about the problem of subjective judgment, and Democritus asserting that it is only by convention that we can talk about sweet, bitter, hot, and cold, "but in reality there are only atoms and the void," you know you're in a different kind of world than that of blind mimetic belief.

I am not, I should add, claiming that nonparticipating consciousness is without its problems; indeed, that was the entire point of my book *The Reenchantment of the World*. But it is also the case that there is too much that simply cannot be solved from within a strictly mimetic framework, and this is why we need to ask if the Enlightenment tradition can ever be made to "stick." Reading its late twentieth-century representatives–I am thinking of philosophers such as Peter Singer and John Rawls–I am often frustrated at how naïve they are, because they are clearly talking about how people "ought" to behave (i.e., rationally) and not how they actually behave (i.e., tribally). What planet are you guys on? is the annoyed reaction I frequently have. And yet, this is the crucial point: controlling the excesses of tribal consciousness really does mean taking the Enlightenment tradition seriously, breaking the "trance," and standing outside the particular meme we are caught up in (whatever it is) and evaluating it rationally and empirically. Singer and Rawls don't have any clear ideas on how to get to such a place, and frankly, neither do I. My guess is that force, not reason, will be the deciding factor in a whole host of areas as the twenty-first century wears on. But it's challenging to think about what a non-mimetic path might consist of.

Here is a single example, something I can't really do myself, but at least aspire to. A very long time ago, when I first got interested in Karl Marx, I ran across a biography of the man by Isaiah Berlin. At the time I had no idea who Isaiah Berlin was, but as I was keen to learn more about Marx, I read the book from cover to cover. It was a very sympathetic portrait of the great German philosopher; the author managed to get inside his head, enable you to see the world through Marx's eyes. I came away impressed with Marx as a thinker; really, as a heroic figure. And then I subsequently learned that communism was complete anathema to Berlin, who was a Russian (actually, Latvian) emigré; and that if there was one single political ideology he hated, it was that. I still retain a great admiration for Marx, of course, and confess I have some reservations about the work of Isaiah Berlin in general (see Essay #13). But that is neither here nor there. Given his own mimetic background, it is hard not to regard his portrait of Marx as a type of heroism all its own.

*Captain Alfred Dreyfus was a French Jewish artillery officer falsely convicted of treason in 1894, and sent to the Devil's Island penal colony in French Guiana, where he spent two years in solitary confinement. The real culprit, Ferdinand Esterhazy, was tried and acquitted in 1896 in what amounted to an Army cover-up (including the falsification of documents). In 1898, the famous writer Émile Zola led the public protest against the government, as the "Dreyfus Affair" tore the nation apart. Eventually, all the charges against Dreyfus were dropped, and he was finally exonerated in 1906. All in all, not exactly France's finest hour.

References

Richard Dawkins, *The Selfish Gene* (New York: Oxford University Press, 1976).

Karl Mannheim, *Ideology and Utopia*, trans. Louis Wirth and Edward Shils (New York: Harcourt Brace and Co., 1936).

Marcel Proust, *In Search of Lost Time*, II: *Within a Budding Grove*, trans. C.K. Scott Moncrieff and Terence Kilmartin and rev. D.J. Enright (New York: Modern Library, 2003), pp. 643-44.

26. Tongue in Chic

> I'm in with the in crowd
> I go where the in crowd goes
> I'm in with the in crowd
> And I know what the in crowd knows.
>   –Dobie Gray, "The In Crowd"

For many years now, I have been fascinated by the human desire to be "cool," to be perceived by others as in the know, "hipper" than all the rest. I recall one fellow-student in my dormitory, during my first year at university, writing an essay on the subject for a class in English or sociology. This was in the early years of the sixties, when the work of Vance Packard (*The Status Seekers, The Pyramid Climbers,* etc.) was very much in the air. In any case, this student interpreted the actions of everyone on campus—students, staff, faculty, administration—as attempts to demonstrate that one was more sophisticated than everyone else. He wasn't far off, as it turns out: a student guide to American universities subsequently described the ambience of the place as that of "one-upsmanship."

I was impressed by the analysis of this student's essay because it corresponded to my own experience. Thinking back, it seems to me that virtually every conversation I had or witnessed during those years had as its subtext the desire to impress. Not much of a basis for friendship, of course, and it is not surprising that I never returned to the place, never attended a class reunion, and never kept in touch with anyone from that era.

But it would be wrong to assume that university is where all of this begins. The phenomenon of cliques and in-groups dates at least from high school, which sets the template for all our future relationships. I remember one extremely intelligent student, Roger S., deciding to run for class president one year. There was a school assembly at which each of the candidates had five minutes to present their "platform." After a series of morons in suits talked about how they would institute free coke machines or whatever, Roger got up, dressed in everyday clothing–definitely uncool–and quietly told his audience, "I'm not here to impress you. I don't intend to dress up for you. I have no free gifts to offer you. I'm just going to give you honest student government and a real opportunity for you to participate in it." Roger was the epitome of unchic and was consequently slaughtered at the polls, end of story. (Well, not quite: Roger went on to become Chief of Cardiology at one of the largest medical schools in the country. As for the guy giving out free Coca-Cola, he has long since disappeared from the historical record.)

In a sense, we remain in high school all our lives. This is pathetic, but it finally is what politics, and our social lives, are all about. I recall the wife of a famous psychiatrist–a guru, really–telling me that if she had friends over for dinner, the next week all of the women who had been at her house adopted her style of dress and cuisine. If she then changed these, they followed accordingly. It was as though they believed in a contagion theory of chicness: if they copied her, some of the "glow" would rub off on them. Absurd, yes, but this desire for chicness is no small force in human psychology or history. It's the norm, not the exception.

The truth is that trying to be cool is a behavior that dates from the Paleolithic. When Paleolithic skeletons are dug up from roughly 35,000 years ago, and are found wearing jewelry–beads, pendants, necklaces–what else can this indicate but an attempt to say one is special–in fact, better than others? The same goes for "special" grave sites for the elite. Personal adornment and special grave-yards are about status differentiation–Vance Packard in the Stone Age, one might say. All the evidence points to a new type of personality organization around that time, which made possible culture as we know it, and which also included the need to feel superior to others–in particular, wanting to be *seen* as superior to others. After all, being cool is something that has to be publicly agreed upon; it is essentially other-defined. Which means it is as insub-stantial as gossamer; who or what is cool can change in the twinkling of an eye. But human beings pursue it as if their lives depended on it. In fact, very few human beings manage to escape the lure of superiority. When you meet Zen masters who are proud of their humility (an experi-ence I've actually had), you know, as André Malraux once observed, that "there really is no such thing as a grown-up person."

Chasing status may be puerile, said John Adams, but it nevertheless seems to be hard-wired. In his *Defence of the Constitutions of the United States of America* (1787), he said that history makes it quite clear that man is driven by van-ity, by a desire for social distinction. "We may call this desire for distinction childish and silly, "wrote Adams, "but we cannot alter the nature of man."

As a result, literally anything can be made chic, even garbage. There is a famous scene in Michelangelo Antonioni's film *Blow Up* in which a band leader goes crazy and smashes his guitar to pieces on the stage. The central character (played by the British actor David Hemmings) leaps onto the stage, seizes the guitar "carcass," and runs off with it, pursued by the crowd, who is convinced he is in possession of something extremely valuable. He manages to give them the slip, and standing alone in an alley, trying to catch his breath, looks at this broken piece of guitar. What is it? A useless piece of trash, really. He tosses it on the ground and walks away.

Even the anti-chic can be made chic. A Canadian magazine, *Adbusters*, became somewhat famous for ridiculing the need to be chic. It is now one of the chicest journals around–"underground chic," as it were. If you are not aware of this publication, you are definitely out of it, and not as good as the people who are aware of it and read it on a regular basis. You are leading a diminished, unchic life.

This brings us to the causes of chic. If it really is as frivolous as it looks, why are we all doing it? Why does all of life finally boil down to high school? Alfred Adler, the psychoanalyst whose major concepts were "superiority complex" and "inferiority complex," argued that the two were intimately related: the desire to be superior masked a deep sense of inferiority. If I care that much about being chic, it must be because I know, on some level, that I am terribly unchic. And this feeling of being inadequate, which dates from infancy, can finally never be overcome; which means that chicness is infinite: you can never be chic enough. Malraux was right: we never grow up.

Imported into politics, all of this points to the limit of any egalitarian experiment. Status always manages to sneak in through the back door. Somehow, so-called left-wing writers in the United States (Noam Chomsky excepted; he really is the "real thing"), in their arguments for a just society, compete for influence and visibility, for being *the* important cultural critic. (I know of one case in which a major left-wing guru actually showed up at a lecture hall in a stretch limousine, surrounded by paparazzi.) The apparatchiki of the former Soviet Union all had dachas (villas) near the Black Sea or in the countryside, and got to buy forbidden Western goods at special stores reserved for them alone. In the end, Lao Tzu was right: the only person you want as a leader is the one who is not interested in the job. (Man, that dude was *really* chic.)

I recall, early on in the Clinton administration, the attempt to institute a program that would have involved holding and loving infants for the first three years of their lives. I don't think the Clintons were trying to be chic here; I think they were genuinely committed to the fundamental concept of child psychology, that feeling secure and loved as a child means one will be less likely to be aggressive and competitive as an adult. Of course, the whole thing fell out of sight in less than a month, as the news media moved on to the next trendy topic. But it was a utopian project, in any case: if we are going to have to restructure human child-rearing in order to restructure our politics, we are going to be waiting for a very long time. The yogic idea that social transformation is personal transformation multiplied millions of times sounds good in the ashram, but has very little applicability in the outside world.

"Out of the crooked timber of humanity," wrote Immanuel Kant, "no straight thing was ever made." On the individual level, the antidote to chic is probably a good sense of humor. I mean, there really *is* something hilarious about it all, no? But in social or institutional terms, I don't see that there is very much that can be done. Although lately, I've been working on a movie script, in which a large, dark, unchic force comes out of nowhere and sweeps across the planet, de-chic-ing everything in its path. I think of it as a kind of a reverse horror film. So stay tuned to this station; I'll let you know how it all turns out.

27. The Parable of the Frogs

One who knows "enough is enough" always has enough.
  –*Tao Te Ching*

What does it take to produce large-scale social change? Most historians, if you catch them in an honest moment, will admit that the popular levers of social change, such as education or legislation, are bogus; they don't really amount to very much. What *does* make a difference–and then only potentially–is massive systemic breakdown, such as occurred in the United States in the fall of 2008. It was the greatest market crash since 1929, leading to widespread unemployment (something like 18% of the population, in real–as opposed to official–statistics*) and the loss of billions of dollars in retirement savings. In fact, the crash wiped out $11.1 trillion in household wealth, and this is not counting the several trillion lost in stock market investments. It had been many decades since the middle class found itself in soup kitchens, and yet there they were. In the face of all this, however, very little seems to have changed. Americans are still committed to the dream of unlimited abundance as a "reasonable" goal, when in reality it is (and always has been) the dream of an addict. President Obama's $12 trillion (and growing) bailout and stimulus plan is funneling money into the very banking establishment that gave us the disaster; it rescues the wealthy, not those who really need the money. And while he could have appointed economic advisers such as Paul Krugman and Joseph Stiglitz (both Nobel laureates), who would have attempted to put the nation on a different economic path, he chose instead two traditional neoliberal ideologues, Timothy Geithner and Lawrence Summers, who believe in the very policies that led to the crash. "Change we can believe in" has never sounded more hollow.

The metaphor of addiction is extremely relevant to situations such as these, because addicts always seek to maximize their intake (or behavior) rather than optimize it, even though the former leads to self-destruction. In the face of what seems to be biologically driven activity, reason doesn't have much of a chance. An experiment with frogs some years ago demonstrated this quite clearly. They were wired up with electrodes in the pleasure center of the brain, and could stimulate that center–i.e., create a "rush"–by pressing a metal bar. Not only did the frogs keep pressing the bar over and over again, but they didn't stop even when their legs were cut off with a pair of shears! And if you are going to object that human beings are not frogs, then you obviously haven't been reading the daily newspapers, or observing the behavior of the people around you.

There are, of course, a few intelligent frogs around, ones who struggle to point out the difference between optima and maxima. They don't have much of an audience, as you might expect, but inasmuch as these essays have no pretensions to making a difference in the real world, let's put the matter of popularity aside and concentrate on the ideas instead.

A Question of Values

The first intelligent frog who comes to mind is the anthropologist Gregory Bateson, perhaps most famous for having been married to Margaret Mead. For Bateson, the issue was an ethical one. As he himself put it, "the ethics of optima and the ethics of maxima are totally different ethical systems." The ethics of maxima knows only one rule: more. More is better, in this scheme of things; words such as "limits" or "enough" are either foolish or meaningless. Clearly, the "American Way of Life" is a system of maxima, of indefinite expansion.

But what if the reality of all social systems is that they are homeostatic, which is to say, designed to stay in balance? In that case, said Bateson, the attempt to maximize any single variable (for example, wealth) will eventually push the system into runaway, such that it will destroy itself. To take a physiological analogy, we recognize that the human body needs only so much calcium per day. We do not say, "The more calcium I ingest, the better off I'll be," because we recognize that past a certain point any chemical element becomes toxic to an organism. Yet we seem to be unable to extend this insight to the social or economic realm. We do *not* say, for example, "That company is making too much profit," or "That individual (Bill Gates, Carlos Slim) has too much money for one person," or "The Gross Domestic Product is spinning out of control." Rather than being interested in balance, in stability, we are fascinated by asymptotes–frogs at the bar of pleasure, even while our legs are being cut off. We don't get it, that if you fight the ecology of a system, you lose, especially when you "win."

Maximizing a single variable, wrote Bateson, can seem like an ingenious adaptation, but over time it typically turns into pathology. The saber teeth of a tiger may have had short-range survival value, but this development weakened its flexibility in other situations that proved to be crucial. The "favored" species became so "favored" that it destroyed its own ecological niche, and disappeared. A gain at one level became a calamity at another.

In recent months, two American scholars of the intelligent frog variety began to understand this line of reasoning and to conclude from it that Adam Smith, with his theory of the "invisible hand", was wrong. An early (much milder) version of Gordon Gekko, with his eulogy of greed (in Oliver Stone's 1987 film, *Wall Street*), Smith argued that the collective result of individual self-interest was the prosperity of the whole. But the economist Robert Frank, writing in the *New York Times* (12 July 2009), argues that "traits that help individuals are harmful to larger groups. For instance," he goes on,

> a mutation for larger antlers served the reproductive interests of an individual male elk, because it helped him prevail in battles with other males for access to mates. But as this mutation spread, it started an arms race that made life more hazardous for male elk over all. The antlers of male elk can now span five feet or more. And despite their utility in battle, they often become a fatal handicap when predators pursue males into dense woods.

In the case of the market, says Frank, individual reward structures undermine the invisible hand. "To make their funds more attractive to investors," he writes, "money managers create complex securities that impose serious, if often well-camouflaged, risks on society. But when all managers take such steps, they are mutually offsetting. No one benefits, yet the risk of financial crises rises sharply."

Similarly, U.S. Appeals Court Judge Richard Posner, in *A Failure of Capitalism*, points out that the crash of 2008 was brought about by individual actions that were actually quite rational: bankers and investors pursuing their own interests. Reckless behavior was quite consistent, he says, with being well informed about the risks involved in the context of an economic bubble, and so a great many money managers took those risks. The problem is that what was rational on the individual level was irrational on the collective level, thus leading to a systemic collapse.

We are thus led, quite naturally, from a consideration of optima vs. maxima to the question of individual vs. collective behavior. Which brings me to one of the twentieth century's most intelligent frogs, the biologist Garrett Hardin, who posed the dilemma in a famous essay entitled "The Tragedy of the Commons" (1968). Consider, said Hardin, the example of a pasture shared by local herders. They all understand that the commons belongs to no one in particular, but supports the well being of all and is the responsibility of all. One day, however, one of the herders puts an additional animal out to graze, with the result that he increases his yield. As a result, the pasture is slightly degraded. Meanwhile, other herders come to the same conclusion, and as each makes the rational decision to take advantage of the situation for personal gain, the net result is the overgrazing, and ultimately the destruction, of the common area. In a word, the system favors selfish individuals over those with greater foresight and restraint. Or as Hardin put it, "Freedom in a commons brings ruin to all." Frogs, in a word, are not to be trusted.

How, then, can excess be curbed in a free democratic system? For we can be sure that the intelligent frogs, who are really quite exceptional, are not going to be listened to, and certainly have no power to enforce their insights. True, there are certain countries–the Scandanavian nations come to mind–where for some reason the concentration of intelligent frogs is unusually high, resulting in decisions designed to protect the commons. But on a world scale, this is not very typical. More typical, and (sad to say) a model for many other countries, is the United States, where proposed "changes" are in fact cosmetic, and where the reality is business as usual. In the context of 307 million highly addicted frogs, the voices of the smart ones–Bateson, Frank, Posner, Hardin, et al.–aren't going to have much impact or, truth be told, even get heard.

Of course, authoritarian systems don't have these problems, which is a good indicator of how things will probably develop. Under the name of "harmony," for example, China regulates its citizens for what it perceives to be the common good. Hence the famous one-child policy, introduced in 1979, supposedly prevented more than 300 million births over the next twenty-nine years in a country that was threatened by its own population density. In the case of the United States, the imposition of rules and limits on individual behavior to protect the commons is not, at present, a realistic prospect; the population is simply not having it, end of story. But how much longer before this freedom of choice is regarded as an impossible luxury? In fact, no crystal ball is required to predict the future here. The tragedy of the commons–what Hardin called "the remorseless working of things"–is that a society such as that of the United States won't undertake serious changes even when it is sitting on the edge of an abyss. It has to actually be *in* the abyss before it will entertain such changes; i.e., it has to be faced with no choice at all. It seems unlikely now, but things are probably moving faster than we realize. In terms of population, food, resources, water, social inequality, public health, and environmental degradation, a crunch of the type I am referring to may be only twenty years away.

In Shakespeare's *Two Gentlemen of Verona*, the character Valentine is confronted by an outlaw, who asks him if he is content "To make a virtue of necessity/And live, as we do, in this wilderness?" That may prove to be the only "choice" we have. As Thomas Hobbes put it a few decades after Shakespeare, "Hell is truth seen too late."

*These data are easily manipulated by the government to make things look better than they actually are. For example, individuals collecting unemployment insurance for a few months are officially unemployed, but once that support dries up they are no longer among the statistics of the unemployed even though they are still out of work. In addition, the millions of Americans who are under-employed, who work only a few hours per week, are included in the ranks of the employed. Between 2006 and 2009, 20% of American workers were laid off; 50 million live in real poverty, and many more in a category called "near poverty." Joseph Stiglitz has a good discussion of this in *Freefall* (New York: W.W. Norton, 2010).

References

Gregory Bateson, "The Cybernetics of 'Self': A Theory of Alcoholism," in *Steps to an Ecology of Mind* (London: Paladin, 1973), pp. 280-308.

Garrett Hardin, "The Tragedy of the Commons," was first published in *Science*, Vol. 162 No. 3859 (13 December 1968), pp. 1243-48, and has been anthologized in numerous publications since that time. Available online at www.garretthardinsociety.org.

Chris Hedges, *Empire of Illusion* (New York: Nation Books, 2009).

James Surowiecki, "Inconspicuous Consumption," *The New Yorker*, 12 October 2009, p. 44.

28. What if...?

> We are too impressed with the pattern revealed to
> us...to remember that for the participants history
> is a haphazard affair, apparently aimless, produced
> by human beings whose concern is essentially with
> the trivial and irrelevant. The historian is always
> conscious of destiny. The participants rarely–or
> mistakenly.
> –Ward Moore, *Bring the Jubilee*

There was a time, not too long ago, when historians became interested in what was known as "alternative history." The idea was to pose a speculative, counterfactual scenario and ask, "What if...?" What if John Kennedy had not gone to Dallas in November of 1963, or had survived the attack? What if the Confederacy had won the Civil War, or Germany had been the victor in World War II? What if the USSR had emerged reenergized from the period of "Perestroika," in a new and partially capitalist form? And so on.

Alternative history had a rather short life span within the history profession (to my knowledge), but it has always been a staple of science fiction. The British novelist Kingsley Amis tried his hand at it in *The Alteration* (1976), in which he conceived of a world where the Protestant Reformation failed to catch on, and Europe remained Catholic. In this world, as one might imagine, there were severe limits placed on freedom of expression, as well as on scientific research; but the up side was a society not beset by endless technological innovation, an ever-expanding economy, and a hectic pace of life. It was a civilization that moved at a human pace, one that did not confuse "progress" with a fourteen-hour work day and a surfeit of ultimately pointless electronic toys. Such a window onto the past enables us to view the present–the culture that *did* come to pass–with a much more objective eye. For it may be the case that we do *not* live in the best of all possible worlds, and that the "parallel universe" that got discarded (or rather, that never came to pass) would have been a much better option for those involved, or for their descendants.

One of my favorites in the "alt. history" genre is *Bring the Jubilee*, by Ward Moore, written in 1955 and by now an underground cult classic. The action takes place in a United States–a *northern* United States–that lost the Civil War. Instead of being an industrial powerhouse, it became a kind of backwater, drab and impoverished, while it is the South that is vibrant and culturally alive. This is reality in a mirror, as it were; and it reminds me of the comment made to me some years ago by a German friend. "Many Europeans," he told me, "don't regard the Northern victory as necessarily a good thing. The preservation of the Union led to a dramatic economic expansion and eventually, to the American Empire, with its destructive ambition of dominating the world. A Southern victory would probably have prevented that." Of course, the Fascist attempt to dominate the world was much more pernicious, and then there is the whole question of how long the institution of slavery would have continued sans interference; but my friend's point is nevertheless a valid one, as a host of nations, from Guatemala to Vietnam, can attest to. American history may, in other words, be a positive thing only from an American viewpoint. And in any case, what would have been the ambition of a victorious Confederacy? Probably not imperial, although in *Bring the Jubilee* the author has it invading Mexico and renaming Mexico City "Leesburg," after Robert E. Lee(!).

The point is that we tend to take reality as a given. True, there is a certain historical momentum to events that cannot be overlooked. I don't believe, for example, that the United States would have ultimately been deterred from its imperial trajectory had John Kennedy lived or the Supreme Court not stolen the election for George W. Bush in 2000. In both cases, things were too far gone for any serious changes to have occurred, it seems to me (though granted, Vietnam and Iraq may conceivably been spared the horror we put them through, which would have been no small thing). In a similar vein, the hopes many people (both within and outside of the United States) once placed in Barack Obama have proven to be illusory, as he reveals himself to be little more than Bush with a human face. But continuity is not always the rule; and in his essay "History and Imagination," the British historian Hugh Trevor-Roper makes a good case for alternative history, history "on the cusp":

> At any given moment in history there are real alternatives....How can we "*explain* what happened and *why*" if we only look at what happened and never consider the alternatives....It is only if we place our-

selves before the alternatives of the past...only if we live for a moment, as the men of the time lived, in its still fluid context and among its still unresolved problems...that we can draw useful lessons from history.

It is not that we can arbitrarily choose a different future; history doesn't work that way (and who would the "we" be, in any case?). But what alternative history *can* do is dispel the notion that there is only one right way to live, namely the way we are living now. Not that, for example, a Confederate victory in what some Southerners call "The War for Southern Independence" (or even, "The War of Northern Aggression") would have necessarily given us a better world–slavery having been the obvious dark aspect of the Southern way of life–but that the destruction of a gracious, slow-moving, community-oriented society in favor of a frantic, commercial one is nothing to crow about. Awareness of this (i.e., beyond the geographical boundaries of the South) could be a departure point for political organizing; and at the very least, it opens the door to a different set of behaviors on the individual level, for what that might be worth.

I trust the reader understands that I am not making some declaration here of "The South Will Rise Again!" I'm just selecting one possible example among many, and one could just as easily discuss the Amish of Pennsylvania as a kind of living alternative history in this vein, or perhaps the Shakers, had they survived. As I said in previous essays, I suspect "choice" will be forced upon us, rather than be something we voluntarily undertake. But the value of alternative history is not merely, as Trevor-Roper says, to explain what happened, but more important, to explain what *could* have happened. For we are not living in the best of all possible worlds; this much is obvious. But how much more impoverished would our existence be, if we had no concrete images of worlds that might be significantly better?

29. The Cellular World

I always enjoyed the story of how Ludwig Wittgenstein, after delivering a four-hour lecture to his class in Cambridge on the intricacies of some logical problem, would then go to a movie in town (his favorite genre was the American Western) and sit in the front row, letting the images inundate his overheated brain. Intuitively, it makes sense, the need to turn off the intellect and immerse oneself in fantasy for a while. Now it turns out that it makes scientific sense as well. In her recent book, *The Philosophical Baby*, psychologist Alison Gopnik notes that magnetic imaging studies show that the occipital cortex, which is very active in the infant brain, lights up in adults while they are watching a movie, while the prefrontal lobe shuts down. In short, there is a reversion (if that is the right word) to pre-critical thinking, which adults often experience as a relief from the "tyranny" of the prefrontal cortex. This latter part of the brain is undeveloped in infants, and doesn't fully form in most individuals until they are in their twenties. The implication is that imagination precedes rational analysis; to do art, be creative, or imagine hypothetical worlds, one has to play, to tap into that preverbal substrate of the mind.

In his review of Gopnik's work (*New York Review of Books*, 11 March 2010), Michael Greenberg talks about how elusive and shadowy the infant's consciousness really is. Tolstoy wrote that it was but a slight step from a five-year-old boy to a man of fifty, but a huge distance between a newborn and a five-year-old. Greenberg says of the first five years of life:

> Mysterious and otherworldly, infancy and early childhood are surrounded later in life by a curious amnesia, broken by flashes of memory that come upon us unbidden, for the most part, with no coherent or reliable context. With their sensorial, almost cellular evocations, these memories seem to reside more in the body than the mind; yet they are central to our sense of who we are to ourselves.

Proust immediately comes to mind, of course: the scene with the *madeleine* in *Du côté de chez Swann*, where the taste of the cookie suddenly opens the door to a flood of childhood memories, long forgotten but still latent in the body. "Cellular evocations...central to our sense of who we are to ourselves." If the phrase "human identity" has a meaning, surely this is it. And yet that fundamental cellular identity gets papered over, as it were; as we grow older, we become someone else. But it is not clear that the archaic self ever goes away completely.

In his autobiography, the psychologist Carl Jung tells the story of a man who comes to him for therapy, apparently at the insistence of his wife. The man is dull as a stick: a Swiss high school principal of about sixty years of age, who did everything "right" all his life, and never experienced a moment of ecstasy or imagination. Jung suggests that he keep a record of his dreams, which he does, showing up at the second session with something potentially disturbing. He dreamt that he entered a darkened room, and found a three-year-old infant covered with feces, and crying. What, he asked Dr. Jung, could it mean? Jung decided not to tell him the obvious: that the baby was himself, that it had had the life crushed out of it at an early age, and was now crying out to be heard. Exposing the "shadow" to the light of day, Jung told himself, would precipitate a psychosis in this poor guy; he wouldn't be able to handle the psychic confrontation. So Jung gave him some sort of neutral explanation, saw the man a few more times, finally pronounced him "cured," and let him go.

One wonders if the good doctor did the right thing. Is a living death preferable to a psychotic awakening? On the other hand—and I have a feeling Jung would agree with me on this—aren't we all that man, to some degree? Perhaps not as wigged out, but it may be a question of degree, nothing more. Abandonment of that cellular identity is the abandonment of life itself; the abandonment of the part of ourselves that is in touch with the "miraculous," as some have called it.

A couple of poems come to mind. One is by Antonio Machado (my translation):

> The wind, one clear day, called to my heart
> with the sweet smell of jasmine.
>
> "In exchange for this aroma,
> I want the scent of all your roses."
> "I have no roses; the flowers
> in my garden are gone; they are all dead."

"Then I'll take the tears from your fountains,
The yellow leaves and the withered petals."
And the wind left...My heart bled...
"My soul, what have you done with your poor little
garden?"

Who, upon reading this, can't feel a sense of guilt, a
sense of something having been betrayed, and now faintly
stirring, knocking on the door of consciousness, asking to
be heard, at long last?

The same theme comes up in "Faith Healing," by the
British poet Philip Larkin, which describes a "workshop"
being held somewhere in England by a visiting American
guru. Undoubtedly, he is something of a charlatan; but
even (or especially) charlatans know how to press the right
buttons. The women in the workshop line up to be held by
him for twenty seconds, to hear him ask, *Now, dear child,
What's wrong,* before he moves on to the next person.
Most just come and go, but some start twitching, crying,

> ...as if a kind of dumb
> And idiot child within them still survives
> To re-awake at kindness, thinking a voice
> At last calls them alone...

> What's wrong! Moustached in flowered frocks they
>   [shake:
> By now, all's wrong. In everyone there sleeps
> A sense of life lived according to love.
> To some it means the difference they could make

By loving others, but across most it sweeps
As all they might have done had they been loved.

Larkin goes on to compare this moment to the thaw-
ing of a frozen landscape, a weeping that spreads slowly
through the body—just from the fact of being asked the
question, of having someone recognize that there is even
a question to be asked. As with Machado, it's hard not to
identify with the emotion that is being pulled out of a deep
cellular memory. What is the "poor little garden," if not
the "sense of life lived according to love" sleeping within
us, the cellular memory that never really goes away?

There is, of course, in virtually every society, a
kind of conspiracy to keep that memory out of conscious
awareness. We need to ask why that would be the case; but
meanwhile, it's clear that if it emerges at all, it is by "accident" (the *madeleine* that triggers a kinesthetic memory,
e.g.), or in a therapist's office, or in a dream (or a poem).
If the cellular world is repressed within the individual, it
is also repressed within society. Hence, to study human
psychology is really to study abnormal psychology, and to
study sociology is to really to study a kind of institutionalized insanity; or weirdness, at the very least. But it is hardly
an accident that the two go hand in hand. Observing the
phenomenon in the United States, the psychiatrist Thomas Lewis remarks that "A good deal of modern American
culture is an extended experiment in the effects of depriv-
ing people of what they crave most." "Happiness," he concludes, "is within range only for adroit people who give the
slip to America's values."

A grim assessment, but I doubt there is any way of denying it. Nor is it limited to the United States, of course; if Freud was right, there is no civilization without deep discontent. It just takes a different form in different cultures. And in any case, it is hard to imagine what a society based entirely on cellular memory would be like—although figures such as Rousseau and Nietzsche did their best to sketch it out. True, the results are less than impressive, but one would like to think that more can be done in this direction beyond individual initiative. It is very rare for a society to literally stop, for a moment, and collectively discuss what an authentic way of life might consist of. Indeed, I can barely imagine such a thing, except that it actually happened in France in May/June of 1968, and for those who were privileged enough to have been at the two-month "teach-in" held at the Sorbonne during that time, it was like breathing oxygen. What is man? What is the good life? What are we doing here? And: Why aren't we asking ourselves these questions all the time?

"Come my friends," wrote Alfred Lord Tennyson; "'Tis not too late to seek a newer world."

What a thought.

Provenance of Articles

Note to the Reader: Most of these essays first appeared in Spanish translation, as indicated below.

1. "To See Ourselves as We Are Seen" originally appeared in a shorter version in the monthly supplement *Hoja por hoja*, published by *Reforma* (Mexico City), Vol. 12 No. 137 (October 2008), p.5 ("Vernos como nos ven").

2. "conspiracy vs. Conspiracy in American History" was posted at *Cyrano's Journal Online* on 24 November 2008 (www.bestcyrano.org/cyrano) and subsequently published in *Parteaguas* (Aguascalientes, Mexico), Vol. 5 No. 16 (Spring 2009), pp. 95-98 ("conspiración *vs.* Conspiración en la historia de los Estados Unidos").

3. "Rope-a-Dope: The Chump Factor in U.S. Foreign Policy" was posted at *Cyrano's Journal Online* on 4 February 2009 (www.bestcyrano.org/cyrano) and subsequently published in *SP Revista de Libros* (Mexico City), Vol. 2 No. 13 (April 2009), pp. 5-7 ("*Rope-a-Dope:* El factor de la credulidad en la política exterior de Estados Unidos").

4. "How to Get Out of Iraq" first appeared in *Parteaguas* (Aguascalientes, Mexico), Vol. 4 No. 13 (Summer 2008), pp. 94-96 ("Cómo salir de Irak o el futuro del imperialismo norteamericano").

5. "Locating the Enemy: Myth vs. Reality in U.S. Foreign Policy" was originally given as the Annual Grace A. Tanner Lecture on Human Values at Southern Utah Uni-

versity on 6 March 2007, and then published as a bound pamphlet by SUU in October of that year. The Spanish translation also appeared in 2007, published by Sexto Piso Editorial, Mexico City ("Localizar al enemigo: Mito versus realidad en la política exterior de los Estados Unidos").

6. "The Real Gold" was published in the journal of the Fondo de cultura económica, *La Gaceta* (Mexico City), No. 430 (October 2006), pp. 17-18 ("El verdadero oro").

7. "Ik Is Us: The Every-Man-for-Himself-Society" first appeared in *Parteaguas* (Aguascalientes, Mexico), Vol. 3 No. 11 (Winter 2008), pp. 81-82 ("Somos los Ik: La sociedad de 'cada quien para su santo'").

8. "The Black Hole of Bethesda" first appeared in *La Vanguardia* (Barcelona), "Opinión" section, 21 August 2005, p. 23 ("¿Empieza el declive en Estados Unidos?") and subsequently in *Parteaguas* (Aguascalientes, Mexico), Vol. 2 No. 8 (Spring 2007), pp. 79-80 ("El hoyo negro de Bethesda").

9. "Massacre at CNN" was originally published in *Parteaguas* (Aguascalientes, Mexico), Vol. 3 No. 9 (Summer 2007), pp. 105-7 ("Masacre en la CNN").

10. ""The Structuralists" first appeared in *SP Revista de Libros* (Mexico City), Vol. 3 No. 30, pp. 42-45 ("Los estructuralistas").

11. "A Show About Nothing" first appeared in *Parteaguas* (Aguascalientes, Mexico), Vol. 4 No. 15 (Winter 2009), pp. 81-83 ("Seinfeld: un programa que no se trata de nada").

12. "Spheres of Influence" was first published in *SP Revista de Libros* (Mexico City), Vol. 3 No. 27 (July 2010), pp. 43-44 ("Esferas de influencia").

13. "Democracy in America" first appeared in *SP Revista de Libros* (Mexico City), Vol. 3 No. 28 (August 2010), pp. 40-41 ("La democracia en América").

14. "Love and Death" originally appeared in *Parteaguas* (Aguascalientes, Mexico), Vol. 4 No. 14 (Fall 2008), pp. 97-98 ("Amor y muerte").

15. "The Lure of Other Worlds" was first published in *Parteaguas* (Aguascalientes, Mexico), Vol. 5 No. 19 (Winter 2010), pp. 93-96 ("La tentación de otros mundos").

16. "Ways of Knowing" first appeared in *Parteaguas* (Aguascalientes, Mexico), Vol. 5 No. 18 (Fall 2009), pp. 81-82 ("Formas de conocer") and was also posted at www.escapeintolife.com on 13 January 2010.

17. "Is There Life After Birth?" was first published in a bilingual version in Diego Luna (ed.), *Abel* (Mexico City: Producciones Pingüino, 2010), pp. 145-57.

18. "Be Here Now" was originally published in *SP Revista de Libros* (Mexico City), Vol. 2 No. 18 (September 2009), pp. 40-41 ("Sé aquí ahora").

19. "Fate" first appeared in *SP Revista de Libros* (Mexico City), Vol. 2 No. 19 (October 2009), p. 44 ("Destino").

20. "The Moral Order" was posted at *Cyrano's Journal Online* on 2 March 2009 (http://showcase.bestcyrano.org/) and subsequently published in *SP Revista de Libros* (Mexico City), Vol. 2 No. 15 (June 2009), pp. 43-44 ("El orden moral").

21. "How Chic was My Progress" was posted at *Cyrano's Journal Online* on 13 May 2009 (http://showcase.bestcyrano.org/) and *Daily Kos* on 15 May 2009 (www.dailykos.com).

22. "A Month in Xela" originally appeared in *SP Revista de Libros* (Mexico City), Vol. 3 No. 23 (March 2010), pp. 32-33 ("Un mes en Xela").

23. "The Hula Hoop Theory of History" was posted at *Cyrano's Journal Online* on 15 April 2009 (http://showcase.bestcyrano.org/) and subsequently published in *SP Revista de Libros* (Mexico City), Vol. 2 No. 14 (May 2009), pp. 40-41 ("La Teoría de la historia del aro hula-hula").

24. "The Asian Road to Victory" was posted at *Cyrano's Journal Online* on 9 February 2009 (www.bestcyrano.org/cyrano) and subsequently published in *Parteaguas*

(Aguascalientes, Mexico), Vol. 5 No. 17 (Summer 2009), pp. 85-88 ("La vía asiática a la victoria").

25. "Tribal Consciousness and Enlightenment Tradition" first appeared in *SP Revista de Libros* (Mexico City), Vol. 2 No. 16 (July 2009), pp. 42-44 ("Conciencia tribal y tradición ilustrada").

26. "Tongue in Chic" was first published in *SP Revista de Libros* (Mexico City), Vol. 2 No. 21 (December 2009-January 2010), pp. 58-59 ("Haz chic").

27. "The Parable of the Frogs" was first published in *SP Revista de Libros* (Mexico City), Vol. 2 No. 20 (November 2009), pp. 44-45 ("La parábola de las ranas").

28. "What if...?" first appeared in *SP Revista de Libros* (Mexico City), Vol. 3 No. 22 (February 2010), pp. 30-31 ("¿Qué tal sí...?").

29. "The Cellular World" was originally published in *SP Revista de Libros* (Mexico City), Vol. 3 No. 25 (May 2010), pp. 40-41 ("El mundo celular"), and was also posted at www.escapeintolife.com on 22 August 2010.

ABOUT THE AUTHOR

Morris Berman is well known as an innovative cultural historian and social critic. He has taught at a number of universities in Europe and North America, and has held visiting endowed chairs at Incarnate Word College (San Antonio), the University of New Mexico, and Weber State University. Between 1982 and 1988 he was the Lansdowne Professor in the History of Science at the University of Victoria, British Columbia. Berman won the Governor's Writers Award for Washington State in 1990, and was the first recipient of the annual Rollo May Center Grant for Humanistic Studies in 1992. In 2000 *The Twilight of American Culture* was named a "Notable Book" by the *New York Times Book Review*. Other published work includes *Dark Ages America* (2006), *Why America Failed* (2011), and a trilogy on the evolution of human consciousness: *The Reenchantment of the World* (1981), *Coming to Our Senses* (1989), and *Wandering God: A Study in Nomadic Spirituality* (2000). Dr. Berman has done numerous radio and television interviews in Europe, the United States, and Asia, and in recent years has lectured in Australia, Colombia, Germany, Mexico, Venezuela, and New Zealand. During 2003-6 he was Visiting Professor in Sociology at the Catholic University of America in Washington, D.C., and Visiting Professor in Humanities at the Tecnológico de Monterrey, Mexico City, during 2008-9. His volume of poetry, *Counting Blessings*, appeared in 2011.